I'M *STILL* THERE
FOR YOU, BABY

good question!

I'M ^STILL THERE FOR YOU, BABY

THE ENTREPRENEUR'S GUIDE TO THE GALAXY

VOL. 3

NEIL SENTURIA

blackbird
VENTURES

LA JOLLA, CALIFORNIA

Copyright © 2017 Blackbird Ventures
978-0-9831704-5-7
ebook 978-0-9831704-6-4

Published by Blackbird Ventures
2223 Avenida de la Playa
Suite 206
La Jolla, CA 92037
www.imthereforyoubaby.com
baby@imthereforyoubaby.com
(858) 754-3201

Publishing consulting and product development:
BookStudio, LLC., www.bookstudiobooks.com

Cover design: Don Hollis
Book design: Charles McStravick
Author photo: Brent Haywood

PRINTED IN THE UNITED STATES OF AMERICA

DEDICATION

It is common for a dedication to be short and to name a few of your children (at least the ones you know about) as well as thank your parents who made it all possible— and if you are still happily married (as I am) then you also name your wife who put up with you during the long hours that you slaved away shaping each syllable (with a word-burning pencil).

I think I will take a different tack. I am going to dedicate the book to Ms. Nicole Rockstead. Ms. Rockstead has been my "assistant" for 24 years. The term assistant is a wild misnomer. She has been the quintessential consigliere who has guided me for more than two decades. She was Siri before there was a Siri.

As I age, I can barely remember what I had for breakfast, but in the matter of business and people and relationships, Ms. Rockstead is my "IBM Watson." I say, "Nic, who was the guy who sort of looked like Al Pacino, was wearing that awful yellow shirt and came to the meeting early. I need to . . ." and by that time she has sent me his email, telephone, and a short dossier on what he said and when and to whom—even if it was two years ago. But beware all who enter my office: if you piss off Ms. Rockstead, you are DOA. She is all things Scylla and Charybdis, a true beauty with a charming style and a dulcet tone, always anxious to be helpful, but when annoyed can make Cerberus look like a house pet. So here is the best and final rule—the rule of all rules. To be successful in life, you need only two things—a great wife and a great assistant. If your business is tilting at windmills (and that is what entrepreneurship is all about), then get yourself a Sancho Panza—and marry Dulcinea.

CONTENTS

INTRODUCTION

This is Vol. 3 in the *I'm There for You, Baby: The Entrepreneur's Guide to the Galaxy* series. It is a collection of the best articles that I have written for the *San Diego Union-Tribune* over the last few years.

I am fascinated by the study of entrepreneurship. What that really means is that I am fascinated by the study of people, their decision-making, their behaviors, and how they chase the "stuff that dreams are made of."

I have begun to think that a compilation like this may be more valuable to the budding entrepreneur than a "how-to" book—there are 290 of those. I am hopeful that in reading these stories, entrepreneurs will find a kernel of wisdom or truth that will be highly relevant to where they are in their process and their current adventure.

— NEIL SENTURIA

AMERICA IS THE LAND OF SECOND CHANCES

APRIL 13, 2015

Second chances.

Politics, finance, marriage, careers. America thinks of itself as the land of redemption, rebirth and reinvention.

As my regular readers know, I have spoken several times about entrepreneurship to inmates at the Miramar Brig. This adventure started two years ago when Marshea, the fiancée of one of the soldiers interned there, contacted me, and said that her fiancé, Sgt. Paul Quevedo, read our column and wanted to invite me to speak as part of the re-entry program. Of course, I said "yes"—how could I turn down a captive audience?

Well, Quevedo was released in March and was going back to Chicago to attend DePaul University to get his degree under the GI Bill. He plans to study real estate and finance. He was leaving town in 48 hours (I think the phrase is "blowing this pop stand"), and so Barbara and I took Marshea and him to a nice lunch the day before he left.

Here is his story. Paul grew up in Chicago near Roberto Clemente Academy (the tough side of Chicago) and decided at the age of 15 that he wanted to be a Marine. He had to wait until graduating from high school at 17. He did his combat training in San Diego, where he learned to fix helicopters. He had an initial six-year tour of duty, including time in Okinawa, Japan, and South Korea, and he married a Japanese woman. He re-enlisted and served part of his second tour in Iraq but did not participate in combat there.

And then he got divorced and made the classic bad decision to both use drugs and sell them. His ex-wife was angry and turned him in to his commanding officer and he ended up in the brig—for three and a half years. His day job there was cutting hair. He was the brig barber of Seville, but when he wasn't trimming, he was reading books—lots of books. His favorite was *Think and Grow Rich* by Napoleon Hill.

At lunch, we were struck by his honesty and humility. He admits all his bad choices, and I am sure he will never make them again. He met Marshea in 2010, and they plan to get married in Chicago next year. She works for a large retailer, and during their time together, before the brig, they started a hip clothing line. The stirrings of entrepreneurship.

Here are Quevedo's own words: "It's a time to search yourself and see what's bothering you, your insecurities, why you feel the way you do about certain things; don't waste time, even though they are controlling you." He said he was up for parole a year ago, but the "paperwork got fouled up and they never saw the report about my being admitted to college and the letters of recommendation." And so he had to serve an extra nine months.

Quevedo is stoic about some of the injustices and deeply resolved to make a successful life. I am humbled by what he has had to overcome, and I find myself being hugely aware and grateful for the privileges I had early on in my own life. We all know the phrase "there but for the grace of God, go I."

In one of my current companies, we are facing an interesting second-chance issue. A former employee who was fired for a major drug abuse has asked to come back. He has completed treatment and is repentant. He promises to never make that mistake again. He has skills that we can use, and after some serious discussion and very strong limitations, we agreed to rehire him on a trial basis. But it was not a slam-dunk decision—there was serious debate.

I think of my own life. I have been given second chances. And what I can tell you is that some of them were gifts—it was not that I had an absolute right to a second chance. Grace and forgiveness. After all, this is just after the Easter and Passover season.

RULE #397

When blinded by the light, get very dark sunglasses, go see your opthamologist and look again.

AGRI-BIOTECH ENTREPRENEUR KEEPS BUSY WITH TWO VENTURE FUNDS

APRIL 20, 2015

Most biotech entrepreneurs are not known for their quick wit and humor. But I know one who could easily sit in for Jon Stewart or Jimmy Fallon any day of the week.

Meet Jerry Caulder. Often referred to as the father of agricultural biotechnology, he is without question one of the most visionary and hilarious of his breed, and when I heard that he was currently involved with two venture funds, I called him up to verify the information. His answer was: "I'm only 73; it takes more than one fund to keep me going."

In 1984, Caulder moved to San Diego, where he became the chairman and CEO of Mycogen, then a startup plant sciences company. After an initial public offering, in 1998, it was sold to Dow Sciences for more than $1 billion market cap.

Now he spends his time as managing director of Kapyon Ventures, which develops technology spun out from global research institutes in the plant science area, and chairman of Finistere Ventures, a more traditional fund. Both are focused on the development of companies that hope to transform modern agriculture by increasing productivity and nutrient use efficiency.

Jerry, who grew up in the upper part of the Mississippi Delta, is hard to pin down to one topic at a time, so the interview was wide ranging and included his colleague Han Chen, whom he calls the "smartest person I've ever worked with."

I asked Caulder why he is still so engaged when he could spend all of his time playing golf.

His answer: "My father always said live life like you'll die tomorrow and learn as if you will live forever. My father was a sharecropper and also was one of the brightest guys I've ever known. My parents were hardworking people who knew that education was the way out of poverty."

He earned a Ph.D. at the University of Missouri that provided a scholarship and a research-teaching position. Next, he joined chemical giant Monsanto in St. Louis, where he managed commercial and product development. That led to his involvement with Mycogen in San Diego.

He believes that San Diego is a good place for startups but worries about the regulatory climate and state taxation policies for the long-term.

"Science doesn't have any borders. Companies go where they can raise money and stay where they are appreciated," he said.

The establishment of Kapyon came out of time he spent in New Zealand, where there were a lot of promising technologies and scientists who weren't interested in commercialization. "I suggested that they spin out the technology, and we would establish companies in the U.S. where the market is bigger. (New Zealand's population is only 4.5 million.) The fund was started with $9 million in 2005.

"We thought that there had to be a better way of getting technology out of universities and research institutes. Traditionally you license the technology, you start a company, you end up with about 100 employees, and you reduce the technology to practice, and then you sell the company. What we do is let the scientists continue their research at the university, they get funded and then when the technology is ready for prime time, they get their stuff spun out, without having to write grants," he said.

Finistere was started with a $40 million fund in 2005 and closed on another $150 million in February. The focus is investments in the "impossible" across the agricultural and food value chains.

The ultimate vision is big. "We are facing very real problems—drought, climate change, increasing population, decreased arable land—that have very real solutions—from biotech and not just what we are working on—that unfortunately are being stifled by a very unrealistic fear among the general public. We want choices in our food, which I support. However, when we demonize technologies that can feed the world, not just the most affluent cities, we are slowly taking away those choices from the next generation," said Chen, managing director of Kapyon Ventures. "Water is our most important resource, more so than oil. I hope that necessity will open up a very transparent and ultimately collaborative conversation in society around the role that biotech will and needs to play."

The Delta is home to the blues, to William Faulkner and to Jerry Caulder. Good company.

RULE #399

You are what you eat.

STARTUP AIMS TO BROADEN WORLD FOR VISUALLY IMPAIRED

JUNE 1, 2015

Seeing is believing.

Many entrepreneurs get the idea for their company from their personal experience. When Suman Kanuganti and Yuja Chang, San Diego engineers, had a longtime friend, Matt Brock, who lost his sight, the three started talking about how they could use Google Glass (a type of wearable technology) to help blind and visually impaired people become more mobile and independent.

The conversation began in January 2014 and by April, Kanuganti and team had developed a prototype that involved utilizing Google Glass along with personalized assistance from a remote agent. This was the beginning of Aira. At the time, Kanuganti was a student in the MBA program at UC San Diego's Rady School of Management, where he learned about the lean startup model, and the concept was also being introduced at Intuit, where he was a development manager. Lean startup emphasizes the importance of talking with customers early in the product development process, building a minimal viable product and then getting customer feedback before making something more complex.

Importantly, Aira was Kanuganti's second startup. The first one had failed, he said, because the team had focused on developing cool technology and hadn't done enough research on regulatory issues that turned out to be significant. This time, he did a lot of market research that included reaching out to organizations like the Foundation Fighting Blindness, the host of an annual "Dining in the Dark" event. At their May 2014 dinner in San Diego, he demonstrated the product, and serendipitously, the speaker was Larry Bock, one of our favorite entrepreneurs, the founder of many successful biotech companies including Illumina and a venture capitalist. Bock is also visually impaired.

"I have tried every assisted device you can imagine and with many of them you stand out like a sore thumb," Bock said. "Google Glass is the first inconspicuous device for the vision-impaired community, and so when I met Suman and Yuja, I was interested in what they were doing."

Over the next few months, Bock conducted due diligence that included meeting with TechTalk, a group of 30 tech-savvy blind people in Los Angeles. "I had thought that this would be useful to people who had a late-onset vision problem like myself so they knew what it was like to see the world. What came out of this was that congenitally blind people wanted it just as much." He also personally tested the product.

"For a person with my type of condition, I order the same thing every time at Chipotle because I can't see the overhead menu. With Aira, the agent can read the menu to me. Over time, the agents can learn my preferences so they know how to narrow the choices," he said. "GPS gets you to the door but can't tell you where the door is, and it's useless indoors. Aira can also help with recognizing friends, finding open seats on a bus, and looking for queues."

In January, Bock Family Ventures, Lux Capital and ARCH Venture Partners invested $325,000 in a seed round, and Bock became executive chairman. In addition, the company has received a $300,000 research grant from Bock.

Aira agents, who can work from anywhere with an Internet connection, use a real-time interactive cloud-based dashboard that can process live data streams from cameras, GPS and other sensor systems from wearable platforms such as Google Glass and Vuzix. The revenue plan is a subscription model based on usage.

According to their market research, about 20.6 million people in the U.S. report that they have trouble seeing, even with glasses or contacts, or they are blind. In San Diego, they believe there are about 75,000 visually impaired or blind people. Ultimately, they also plan to develop their own hardware that will be less expensive than Google Glass because it will be more tailored to the needs of their customers.

This is a busy time for the company. In early May, Aira was one of 26 startups and one of the five launch-stage companies accepted into the EvoNexus incubator out of 212 applicants. The next big step is the launch of a beta trial in July with at least 100 users.

"We understand user scenarios and the type of help that can offer. The beta test will help us define the proper ratio of agents to users; we'll learn how often people use the service and how much we can charge," said Bock, who added that they still have room for additional people in the trial.

RULE #413

"Vision is the art of seeing what is invisible to others."

—JONATHAN SWIFT

EX-UCSD PLASTIC SURGEON TAKES ON FDA REGULATION

AUGUST 24, 2015

Breasts. That is what is called a provocative lead. But the truth is that breast implants are a complex subject, and Dr. Jack Fisher has a lot to say on the topic.

After retiring as head of the division of plastic and reconstructive surgery at UC San Diego for 20 years, Fisher could have spent his time fishing and playing golf. Instead, he earned a master's degree at UCSD in U.S. political and economic history and began the next chapter of his life—doing in-depth research on how we regulate our food, drug and medical device industries and concluding that our current system impedes innovation and entrepreneurship.

(**NOTE:** Imagine coming to the conclusion that the system is broken and doesn't promote innovation. Who would ever have thought that?)

In his recently published book, *Silicone on Trial: Breast Implants and the Politics of Risk*, Fisher focuses on the hysteria in the 1990s over silicone breast implants, and he offers recommendations on how the Food and Drug Administration should be changed to better serve patients. Medical device companies spend millions seeking approvals from the government, but Fisher learned that "government regulation is a political process and not a scientific one, even when the product is based on technology."

Let me remind you of 1990, when CBS-TV correspondent Connie Chung's story about the "dangers" of silicone breast implants raised alarms throughout the country. According to Fisher,

Chung's story was based on interviews with only four women and two medical experts who were later disqualified as witnesses in American courtrooms because of fraudulent qualifications. "Omitted entirely was mention of a clinical study showing no increase in breast cancer among implanted women," said Fisher.

Fisher notes that what happened next was a wave of terror, and when the results of an actual patient survey were released, the media largely ignored it. In 1992, FDA commissioner David Kessler called for a moratorium on the use of silicone gel breast implants. A slew of lawsuits were filed, and surgeons were suddenly limited in the choice of available devices, even for breast reconstruction following mastectomy. Not until 1999 did silicone devices receive a "full pardon," and it was from the National Academy of Science's Institute of Medicine, not the FDA. But this came too late to help the silicone industry that had spent billions of dollars fighting lawsuits and paying what he believes were phony claims, Fisher writes.

"While I can hope this book might provide comfort for all prior implant recipients, I would like the data to be equally valuable to women considering breast implants for the first time," said Fisher.

In his book, Fisher offers several recommendations on how to correct the problems that plague the Food and Drug Administration. He begins with the premise: "We overreact to risk in America. We should rely more on scientific evidence. For example, restricting breast implants on the basis of a few cases of illness that later proved to be coincidental is not rational regulation. Sometimes we confuse coincidences with cause and effect."

Currently, the FDA approves for both safety and efficacy both drugs and devices, and naturally it takes much longer to approve efficacy. Fisher believes that we should move to the European model—approve drugs and devices for safety and then measure efficacy after a drug gets to the marketplace.

(**NOTE:** Sort of like the lean startup model.)

He quotes former FDA commissioner Margaret Hamburg, who said, "The FDA is relying on 20th-century regulatory science to evaluate 21st-century medical products." He also notes that former FDA director Henry Miller has recommended using the successful model of the nonprofit Underwriters Laboratories (UL), which tests and certifies thousands of consumer products (some of them hazardous) at "a fraction of the cost the FDA imposes."

"The challenge for policy makers and regulators is to find a balance between risk estimates and statutory limits, between product innovation and market barriers, between unanticipated outcomes and rational compensation for avoidable hazards," Fisher concludes.

The measurement of real risk is a challenge across all sectors, from manufacturing to drugs to personal privacy to crossing the street at rush hour. And how to assess risk and then balance risk with regulation has massive impacts on the economics of your adventure.

RULE #432

Risk is not a board game anymore.

BACK TO THE BRIG: SHARING STORIES OF FAILURE WITH A CAPTIVE AUDIENCE

AUGUST 31, 2015

Back to the brig.

Getting invited back to "do Miramar" is a little like your agent telling you that Letterman wants you back to do five minutes of stand-up, except in this case it is 90 minutes on entrepreneurship to 75 prisoners. And, as always, it is nice that I get to leave the brig when it is done. I am sure one of these times they will throw away the key.

The military has a program that encourages and teaches business skills to their inmates, since all of them eventually get out and all of them desire to be integrated into civilian life again and either get jobs or start companies. Recently, I was privileged to talk to "my gang" for the fourth time, and I can tell you that they are without question highly interested and focused and intelligent and ready to take charge of their lives.

As a note, the recidivism rate at the brig is less than 2 percent. That shows the value of providing programs and education.

We discussed many of the big ideas that readers of this column know by heart, as well as a couple of personal war stories, including, but not limited to, a recent failure I was involved in. You learn more from the failures than you do from the successes.

One of the themes this time was "I waited too long." We all know that the hard decisions in companies are often uncomfortable and even though we recognize the issue, there is still a distinct tendency and desire to avoid unpleasantness. This is a human trait, not unique to entrepreneurs. I recently fell victim to this disease—the "I hope if I look the other way, it will magically go away and everything will be fine again" syndrome. (Find me a biotech that can solve that disease, and I am the lead investor.)

I waited too long to fire the CEO, and when the fan got hit, the ensuing issues were ugly and much of the pain and the losses could have been avoided if I had trusted my gut earlier and been willing to deal with the hard conversation when I knew I should have.

(**NOTE:** Read *The Hard Thing About Hard Things,* by Ben Horowitz.)

In the same vein, I recently had a "stock vesting" issue in another company. The CEO finally faced that we had to terminate an employee, but by waiting a year too long to do this, he created conflict among the other employees who saw the unfairness of the situation, while at the same time creating unnecessary dilution for the whole company.

I have another company with a CEO who needs to have an unpleasant conversation with the lead investor. Again, my advice is to face it and do it now. And while we are on the subject of unpleasant conversations, let's go back to the brig. One of the issues the prisoners have to deal with when they get out is their record. In certain cases, they have a dishonorable discharge; in other cases, they have a record as a felon.

I was asked, "What do you tell a prospective employer?" The answer is: Tell the truth and tell it early in the interview. There is no place to run, no place to hide; do it upfront. You made a mistake; put it on the table. I do not believe that fact alone will disqualify you for a job. I am always a fan of and a supporter of the second chance. If at the pearly gates, I am asked do I want justice or mercy—no contest, I will take mercy every time.

And finally on the subject of incarceration and educational programs, in the past year, I have also been contacted by several

East Mesa detention facility inmates who read this column. They have asked me to come and talk to them. Unfortunately, although I have tried several times, I have been unable to get anyone in the Sheriff's Office to respond to my request. However, I will continue the effort.

RULE #303

Sometimes it is easier to get out of jail than it is to get in.

SPOUSES TEAMING UP TO RUN A BUSINESS CAN BE RECIPE FOR SUCCESS

OCTOBER 12, 2015

"Honey, I shrunk the kids" is not as disturbing in some marriages as "Honey, I burned the chicken, dropped the tiramisu on the floor and the kitchen is currently on fire." The combination of working with your spouse and trying to build a successful restaurant can be a recipe for disaster. The restaurant industry is littered with failures, and the stress of a startup can damage even the best relationship.

(**NOTE:** I have invested in two restaurants. One was a smash, and the jury is still out on the other, which just happens to be run by a husband-and-wife team.)

I met Amanda Caniglia, co-founder of the Bella Vista Social Club & Caffe, through her role hosting brainstorming meetings for the Mesa Project, an initiative that explores how to better brand and market our region's innovation economy. Bella Vista is on the second floor of the Sanford Consortium for Regenerative Medicine, across the street from the main UC San Diego campus. It is a modest space that opens onto a giant and gorgeous deck with an ocean view.

"Our goal was to create an environment, a piazza, where people can come and be comfortable. People collaborate better when they have food and alcohol. It's how friendships and relationships are formed," said Amanda, who started Bella Vista with her husband, Nico. "In San Diego, we lack good gathering places."

Amanda and Nico were both working at a restaurant in Little Italy when they met. Amanda was in her car, had the right of way and abruptly was cut off by a guy who hit the horn, gave her the finger and took the last parking space—and when she finally got inside, late for work? Yeah, of course, the guy was Nico. They were made for each other.

They married in 2006 and their first business foray together was Swieners, a mobile food truck company that primarily worked with craft breweries. Their product was a grilled bratwurst served on a fresh baguette with melted raclette cheese. They also ran a small café on Bankers Hill until they lost their lease.

(**NOTE:** They knew the industry. They had worked in a restaurant. You would be surprised at the number of people who start a business in which they have never worked previously.)

Bella Vista opened in January 2013. Initial capital of $25,000 came from their savings, plus loans from family members and a business partner, who they were able to pay off within six months. For the first year, they continued to operate Swieners in order to pay their bills. They didn't draw a salary and any profits were reinvested into the business. Amanda estimated that they have spent over $100,000 on inventory, equipment, a van for catering, licenses, permits, outdoor patio furniture and expansion of the bar.

(**NOTE:** To open a full restaurant of 3,500 to 5,000 square feet, the cost would be north of $850,000—more like $1.3 million.)

The Caniglias started slowly by offering breakfast and lunch Monday through Friday, then adding brunch on Saturday and

Sunday, and recently a happy hour and dinner during the week. On a typical weekday, Amanda said Bella Vista serves 200 to 300 people at lunch. "Our kitchen was built for a café and is only slightly larger than a walk-in closet."

How does the couple work together and stay married?

"Nico and I divide and conquer. We don't yell at each other. We give each other a lot of space. We have a lot in common but we're also very different. We're both gypsies; we speak several languages. We have similar values but very different personalities," said Amanda.

With a business that is open seven days a week plus a growing catering operation (and a six-year-old son), there is no time off, and Amanda loves it that way. "I don't like to miss a day of work because so many interesting people roll through the café."

RULE #440

Marriage is like a chocolate soufflé. Lots of hot air mixed with sweetness.

WELCOME TO THE ULTIMATUM GAME ON DECISION MAKING

NOVEMBER 2, 2015

Today we are going to play a game. It is called the Ultimatum Game.

Let's pretend that $1,000 shows up in your lap with only one condition as follows. You have to decide how to share it with me. You are going to make me an offer—you can split it with me 50–50 or you can decide to do it any other way you want, e.g., 72–28 in your favor.

And I can then decide to either accept or reject this proposal. If I accept, then the money is split as you suggested, but if I reject your offer (in other words, I deem the proposal "unfair"), then neither of us will receive any of the money. Simple.

Oh no—not so simple. Rational choice theory says that I should accept any amount you offer, because it is all found money to me. It is more than I had when we started. So there is no "rational" reason to reject any offer.

But I have feelings, and so while economically you should only offer me $1, the fact is that the decision of whether to accept or reject has very little to do with the actual dollars and everything to do with "perceived fairness." If you want to delve a bit deeper on this one, study the "Nash equilibrium."

Now, why would I reject an offer? "Altruistic punishment" is a concept that essentially says I will reject an offer to teach you a lesson with the hope that you will behave differently in the future with other people. There appears to be a human unwillingness to accept or endorse perceived injustice.

So let's see how our readership thinks about money. I have started an email account: neilultimatumgame@gmail.com. And you, dear reader, are invited to send me your proposals on how you would split the $1,000 with me. And I will publish the results. This concept is sharply in focus in my current life, as I am the lead negotiator for a complex and high-value transaction in which the elements are similar. If we do not sign the deal as proposed, the new buyer will walk and the deal will crater (or so we are led to believe by the founder/promoters). If we do sign the deal, we will get something, but not what we think we should, while the "bad guys" get the vast majority of the loot—essentially we would get 15 cents and they would get 85 cents.

We said to them, "We will sign if you give us 30 cents and you can keep 70 cents—and all the cents that will continue to accrue to the company thereafter. All the future monies are yours; you do not have to share them with us. And there are many cents left to be earned, but we don't want to stick around and wait."

That is code for we are not that trusting that we will ever see the future cents. (There are milestones and options and spin moves that lower the likelihood, in our opinion.)

For additional insight into how to act in your own best interests, you might also look at the famous study known as the "prisoner's dilemma."

In the end, the dissident shareholders held their righteous ground, but the founders were able to persuade the buyer to close the deal around them. Now we will hope their future spin moves spin our way. As you can see, shifting sands make different alliances.

The subtext of this column is that decision making should be driven by math—simple numerical calculations—but often it is not. If you aspire to rational man behavior, then your decisions should be driven by computational economics.

I am also acting as the lead for a venture financing of one of my companies. The initial conversation at the board was all about dilution, amount of dough, pre-money valuation and greed, but in the end it was simple: Do you want to be rich or do you want to be king? Take the smart money (and the lower valuation), because it comes with a chance to build a much bigger company.

I think math as a decision tool is underrated. It should drive almost all your rational man decisions, whether cost of customer acquisition, business model, burn rate or gross margin. There is the wonderful joke about the merchant who only loses a penny on each sale, but then assumes he can make it up on volume.

How would you share $1,000 with me?

RULE #442

Rational economics precedes cooperative behavior.

DO YOU BET ON THE PRODUCT OR THE PEOPLE BEHIND IT?

NOVEMBER 16, 2015

Objects in your rearview mirror are not only closer than they appear, they are also more obvious. That is why they call hindsight 20-20.

I see lots of deals, and the question I struggle with—like all investors—is "Which are the good ones?" And so we turn one more time to my favorite institution, which would not give me the time of day 45 years ago—Harvard Business School—and Professor Pian Shu, who has some thoughts on how to predict if any idea is really a good one.

She starts with Airbnb. The story is that Brian Chesky, co-founder, takes his idea to seven venture capital firms—five throw him out the door after 15 minutes and the other two don't even return his phone call. After all, why would anyone give the keys to their house to a stranger who might be a serial killer? And today, that goofball idea has a valuation of $10 billion.

With my first startup, it took me three tries with the same VC to get him to invest. We discussed (argued) for six months, but in due course the deal was done. The next day, the day after he invested, he told us to go back out for more money at a valuation that was 50 percent higher—24 hours later. I thought he was nuts. His answer: "Now that we are investors, the company is worth more."

But surprisingly, that turns out to be semi-rational. Shu finds in her studies that "by definition, when an investor makes an investment, it changes the probability of success." Shu goes on to say that when dealing with something truly innovative, it's very difficult to compare it to anything that came before—because there is nothing before. So in looking back on successes (LinkedIn had 20 rejections before getting funded), the question is: was it the idea itself or was it that the investment turned the tide—in other words, does having the "right" investor create a self-fulfilling prophecy? Statistics tell us that the VC brand matters, but more on that another time.

So Shu wanted to find out if you can really predict a good idea. She did a study using 100 mentors who reviewed ideas in a neutral setting, presented in a one-paragraph description in a uniform format. And what happened was that if the mentors coalesced around an idea, it had a 30 percent higher likelihood of success. The mentors proved to be very good pickers, but only in certain areas. They had a high correlation in energy, hardware and medical devices. But when it came to mobile apps and software, they were much less effective.

And the reason appears to be that it is easier to shift in the app/software business—and the infamous "pivot" or shift is really important in building a successful company. Airbnb started out suggesting air mattresses on the floor instead of rooms.

This brings us to the infamous paradigm: Do you bet on the horse or on the jockey? Shu shows us that it depends on which sector. R&D-intensive companies, you bet on the horse; with apps and software, you bet on the jockey.

The next shibboleth to fall is the one that says you need industry expertise to evaluate a deal or an idea. Shu shows that "in the collective," i.e. the wisdom of crowds model, industry expertise is relatively meaningless. The idea shines through. The key is being able to see beyond the idea itself—what could be rather than what is. And not knowing the limitations (not having industry expertise) actually frees the investor to expand his thinking.

So you would think that angel groups (where 50 to 100 people assess the idea and the team) would be more effective than not. But that isn't the case. In fact, the VC model (three to six partners) still statistically wins that battle.

When possible, Shu says, building an MVP (minimum viable product) is the most valuable feature, because then the crowd gets to look at something concrete, not just an idea.

In the final analysis, we have to turn to Yogi Berra, who said, "In baseball, you don't know nothing." The same seems to hold true for investing.

RULE #147

If it were easy, everyone would do it.

CROWD DYNAMICS CAN OFFER UP PLENTY OF FRESH IDEAS

NOVEMBER 23, 2015

The wisdom of crowds. James Surowiecki made this concept famous in his 2004 book. This is not the same as crowdfunding (quite the hot topic today). Rather the thesis argues that the aggregation of information from a group leads to a better "answer" than if made by any single member of that group.

Surowiecki gives the famous example of trying to ascertain the weight of oxen at the county fair. The average of all the guesses was the closest to the actual weight—and closer than any single guess from all the participants.

Crowd dynamics are fascinating in everything from riots in the street to the god-awful wave at ballgames. The crowd has a mind of its own.

So a couple of weeks ago, I challenged my readers to play the ultimatum game (see column from Nov. 2). And what I found was that the "crowd of readers" was very original in their thinking and came up with fascinating and unconventional ways to split the money. The classic is 50–50, but now for some new ideas.

"I will give you 70 percent, but the stipulation is that 60 percent of your money goes into a mutual fund investment and after five years, we split the proceeds 50–50." This guy also offered an email address for a Nigerian prince.

Several readers suggested I take all the money and invest it in a startup—namely theirs. They did not stipulate the pre-money valuation.

(**NOTE:** You can name your price or you can name your terms, but you can't name both.)

Another reader said 50–50 "for the first time, but the next time, much more to me." I responded by telling him there would be no next time.

Another kind lady also went 50–50 and wrote "gratitude, charity and prosperity are a mind-set replacing greed and self-interest." This woman should run for public office.

One woman gave me a complicated real-life negotiation to solve. This reminds me to be careful what I wish for—I may get it.

Another reader wrote a long treatise to explain that if I were a "friend" he would give me 40 percent, but since he figures he will never see me again, he is offering only 33 percent to me, the rest to him. I guess friendship is fungible.

Several said 60–40 my favor, hoping we could do more business together in the future. This leads to another famous paradigm. One party is hopeful for reciprocation, and offers first and generously, but then turns deeply angry when I take the money and run and offer nothing further in return. The retort "that's not fair" echoes loudly down the halls of many grand institutions when they leave the little guy in the lurch.

And finally good old philanthropy did rear its ugly head. Dan Beintema wrote to me, "I will give you $335, but for every dollar you give away, I will double match it up to $665." This fellow understood the multiplier effect of giving—and then I learned that Mr. Beintema is president of the USS Midway Foundation. Duh.

(**NOTE:** Women and tech "upspeak.")

So, as many of you know, I consider myself the poster child for smart, powerful women. (I married one.) And I am their biggest fan.

Well, along come some white male tech billionaires at the DealBook conference and they have something to say on that subject.

Peter Thiel, PayPal, and Chris Sacca, Twitter and Uber, got together recently in Silicon Valley to discuss many things—one of which was women in tech and why there are not more of them in C-level positions. Thiel was marginally clueless but Sacca took a healthy cut at the topic, criticizing the culture for not grooming women better for leadership positions.

"We don't have a culture that teaches girls financial literacy," Sacca said. "We have a princess manufacturing complex." And then he launched one. He said that people in the Bay Area tended toward "upspeak," which is a rising inflection in speech pattern. He says, "Men can get away with it, but women who adopt that speech pattern are not taken seriously."

Seriously! You must be kidding me. You want all women to change their speech inflections in order to be taken more seriously. Seriously? I am up-speechless at the inanity of his comment. You think that is why more women are not in the C-suite. Please!

RULE #444

Watch the movie *Thelma and Louise* and check out their 9mm upspeak.

FOUNDER-CEO NEEDS TO KNOW WHEN IT'S TIME TO GO

JANUARY 4, 2016

Look in the mirror—you're fired.

And thus we have the question of how to know when to transition leadership from the founding chief executive to someone else "who can take us to the next level."

(**NOTE:** Or run the thing into the ground.)

Suren Dutia, a senior fellow with the Kauffman Foundation, has some thoughts on that subject. He says startup founders "are heavily invested in the dream of leading the company."

I know he is correct, and as an investor, I am more inclined to touch this third rail earlier than not. This is the whole "rich vs. king" syndrome, and I explore this area deeply before funding.

When I was CEO and took investor money, I often joked (but with tongue tied behind my back) that I would write my resignation at funding and give it to the board, so they would be able to fire me without any ugliness or hanging on.

(**NOTE:** I have been CEO seven times and was fired twice. The first time I was deeply unhappy and was sure they were making a big mistake—and that company sold for more than $80 million.)

Dutia cites data from Noam Wasserman, Harvard Business School professor, that "less than half of founding CEOs retain their title after three years." And less than 25 percent of the CEOs who had a successful exit resulting from an IPO were founder-CEOs. In other words, hanging around too long might be detrimental to your wealth.

Wasserman goes on to say, "When a founder-CEO stepped down, the value of the company equity increased."

So the real question is why—why is it so hard for the founder to let go? Why is the mirror so clouded?

Dutia says, "Almost 80 percent of founder-CEOs are reluctant to give up control." They confuse their passion with their skills.

I am a consultant to a struggling telecom company and the major investor came to me for advice—and after reviewing the issues, my rather immediate advice was to fire the CEO. And the interesting thing is that the investor himself had been thinking about doing this for 18 months, but was afraid to pull the trigger. He wanted someone else to validate his perception. This is the classic "I waited too long" syndrome.

I see this issue regularly in early-stage investing. Angels talk about someone being "mentorable," but I think what they are really trying to say is "Will he know when to step down—and without a fight—so I don't have to litigate any craziness?"

My own solution of late has been to actively assume the role of executive chairman. This is a term of art that carves out a role more than chairman of the board and less than CEO. There are few main areas of focus—all dealing with external funding. Often, the CEO (which is the case in a biotech I am involved in) is brilliant at science and only moderately skilled in finance. Let people do what they do best.

Another main area for an executive chairman is merger/acquisition/joint ventures and deals. I am funding another company where the CEO is a former Marine sniper (this is one time where severe disagreements could be adverse to my long-term health)— but to his credit, he is totally willing to restructure the corporation, the stock, the compensation, the vesting, etc., because the product is brilliant. I know enough not to touch the product.

My partner and I have a company where the CEO is really the COO, but he is so good at operations and execution that we want him to keep the CEO title. My partner simply "bolsters" him, but stays in the wings. This is an important job—being coach without trying to run on the field and throw the pass. The fact that you can touch something does not mean you should touch it. Part of the executive chairman role is to provide a plan for "CEO success and if needed, succession."

Finally, both Dutia and Wasserman say that if you are going to make a change in the CEO, here are some recommendations: "Don't settle in the hiring process, don't undermine what has been done under the previous administration and don't dawdle—no more than five to six months from start to finish in the hiring and transition."

Executive chairman can be a useful role.

RULE #504

In spite of what you might think, you are not the same as the company.

USING ANGER AS A NEGOTIATING TOOL

JANUARY 11, 2016

My way or the highway.

I spend most of my day negotiating—with everyone from the plumber who can't fix the leak to the entrepreneur who in his lizard brain demands a pre-money valuation of $22 million with no customers and no revenue, or with the angel investors who want a 3x liquidation preference, or with the CEO who wants the legal work to be done by his brother-in-law who got his degree online at Casper the Ghost law school. Oy!

That's what I do. Negotiate. So during this year, I propose to have several columns dedicated to illuminating some of the best thinking on this subject. And the initial effort is centered on how to deal with emotions—specifically anger.

Alison Brooks, a professor at Harvard Business School, thinks anger is a negative emotion. She says, "Bringing anger to a negotiation is like throwing a bomb into the process." But she also notes that many people believe that anger can be a productive emotion and that this perspective comes from a tendency to view the negotiation in competitive terms instead of collaborative ones.

If you have the choice of feeling angry or happy during a negotiation, she finds that anger escalates conflict, "biases perceptions, reduces joint gains, decreases cooperation and increases the rate at which offers are rejected." So you would think anger is not so good, but she shows that more than 60 percent of people "think it makes them more effective and view it as significantly advantageous."

It is wonderful how facts get in the way of beliefs.

So I would like to suggest a slight word modification. Instead of anger, I prefer to demonstrate "mild outrage."

Looking at the other person and saying, "Are you serious, do you really mean that, are you actually going to stand there and tell me—?" And it matters greatly what volume you use in that instance. When I am truly angry, I talk very slowly and very softly. When I am in puffery/performance mode, I am louder, with larger hand gestures. There is a slightly comic effect—a bit of a caricature—which allows me a place to fall back from. I leave myself some room to make fun of myself and then to potentially disarm the other side. But I agree with Brooks—the endgame is always headed ultimately and without exception toward rapport.

Another perspective comes from Stanford professor Margaret Neale, who suggests all negotiations should be viewed as "a problem-solving exercise." In her research, she finds "that when people are drawn into battle, they will sometimes give up too much—even against their best interests—just for the sake of resolution."

This is the divorce lawyer's greatest weapon. Anything for the sake of peace. You can have Aunt Tilly's old Spode china, and I hope you choke on every mouthful.

Neale suggests a few strategies to avoid that outcome. Assess. Do you have enough data to go forward? Do you know enough, can you see the whole chessboard? I recently "lost" a negotiation. The other side's position made no sense, and in a litigation I believe that I would have won hands down. But they were intransigent. In the end, I came to the conclusion that there was something I did not know and could not find out. And I did not have time to find out.

Prepare. Neale argues that "negotiation is not improvisational theater." I politely disagree. While it is wonderful to have a game plan, as Mike Tyson famously has said, "Everybody has a plan until they get punched in the mouth." I think a great teaching tool for CEOs is to take some theater improvisation classes, and I think in every negotiation there is "a moment"—when the right word, phrase, joke or concession seals the deal. Study the *Shark Tank* negotiations. Those guys are really good.

Ask. "He who speaks first loses" is absolutely wrong. Study the concept of "anchoring" and "framing." If I win the toss, I want to receive.

And Neale has one more piece of research that fascinates me. She says homes with precise listing prices (e.g., $789,500) sell for more on average than those with a rounded listing or "value range pricing." My personal experience suggests the opposite and that keeping things "fuzzy" for a while in the discussion works better than a hard number.

But that is what is great about negotiation—we can both be right, at least for a while.

Be prepared, but also be ready to improvise.

RULE #509

You can name your price or you can name your terms— you can't name both.

BREWER'S PATH WAS ANYTHING BUT STRAIGHT

JANUARY 26, 2016

Ninety-nine bottles of beer on the wall.

San Diego has become synonymous with craft beer. We have 115 breweries in the county.

Meet Mike Hinkley, who is the owner of one of them—the Green Flash Brewery. I love his story.

Hinkley grew up in Bensonhurst, Brooklyn. (He was sort of a "good fellow.") His mother was 16 at his birth, and Mike tells me that it took three high schools for him to graduate—barely. "I was not the best student." His parents got divorced, and he went off to join the Navy. He was a machinist mate.

(NOTE: You don't know which life events are actually preparations for the future. That is why you need to embrace all of them.)

During his four years in the Navy, he "grew up"—but not all the way up. He still seemed to have a tendency to get into trouble. His next effort was as a bartender at Kansas City Barbeque ("Top Gun Bar") in downtown San Diego. I asked him if he had any training as a bartender. "No, I just told him I was a bartender."

(NOTE: There is something to be said for self-confidence— and minor omissions of fact.)

He met his wife at the bar and then went off to City College to try to get a degree. He says, "I had to take prerequisites just to get admitted into the class to take the prerequisites." But grades do not define the man and are not a prerequisite to success. He got straight A's and transferred to UC Berkeley and took business and accounting classes, and ultimately became a CPA and went to work for Arthur Andersen in international tax—and of course, hated it.

Lisa, his wife, went to work at Invitrogen and at that moment in time, it looked like the future picture of domestic bliss. But Hinkley hated accounting, so he quit, and bought "a failed bar" in Leucadia. He liked drinking beer in college, so of course, it was perfectly logical to buy a bar.

The next step was a steep one. He "invested" a few hundred thousand dollars in someone else's scheme to build a brewery. I asked him about his due diligence prior to writing the check. His answer: "None." In a month, the money and his partner were gone.

(**NOTE:** The value of doing real due diligence cannot be overestimated. Simply driving by the location does not cut it.)

So after some heated litigation and some more lawyer-lost monies, Hinkley found that what he had won was a warehouse filled with some old pieces of brewing equipment. They could either try to sell the junk or they could try to assemble the stuff and build a brewery (machinist mate). So, in 2001 they decide to "go all in" again.

(**NOTE:** His wife continued to believe in him. Take note, all entrepreneurs: before you do anything, find this wife.)

His motivation to build the brewery was that "I thought it would be cool if my neighbors could buy my beer." Getting rich was not a glimmer in his eye. He was just going to brew up some quality beer. They used a contract brewer with their own recipe, and in November 2002, they sold their first keg. By 2003, they were selling 1,200 barrels per year. (It takes about 5,000 barrels per year to break even.)

2016—Green Flash is now on a roll. It has one brewery in Mira Mesa and is building a new one in Virginia. Green Flash sells 100,000 barrels per year. I asked Hinkley what advice he would give to entrepreneurs. Here is what he said.

1. Focus on the core stuff. You don't need an ERP (enterprise resource planning) system with four employees. Just make great beer or whatever you are making—but make it great.

2. Don't drive bad ideas off the cliff—learn to let go before you crash and burn. (Knowing when to bail out is a strong theme in the entrepreneur game.)

3. Work at a brewery before you start one. Get experience first.

Green Flash has 250 employees today. And oh, yes, the name—he credits his wife, who was sitting in the backyard and watching a sunset. The rest is history—and a history still to be written.

RULE #451

Due diligence is trying to discover that which is hidden.

A LAB GURU'S SHORT COURSE ON GOOD DESIGN

FEBRUARY 8, 2016

"Design is how it works."—Steve Jobs

Great design is hard to categorize, but you know it when you see it.

Now meet Don Norman—not only can he describe it, he has created it. He was educated in electrical engineering at MIT, got his doctorate in mathematical psychology at Penn, taught at Harvard, came to UCSD for 27 years, then left and went to work at Apple and HP. He was a consultant to DARPA and NASA, served on multiple boards, and in his spare time managed to author 20 books on topics in his field. A classic underachiever.

And now he has returned to his roots to lead the UCSD Design Lab. He is the acknowledged guru in the field of usability engineering and cognitive science. And he is a passionate advocate for user-centered design.

So I pressed him to give me the short course in design for dummies. Norman was a consultant after the Three Mile Island nuclear meltdown disaster. Why and how did it happen was his assignment. The initial assumption in many disasters is "user error"—the technicians or the pilot made a mistake. But Norman's work peels back the onion and tries to understand why there was user error. And his thesis is that it is often because of bad design.

Case in point—Three Mile Island had eight knobs on the main panel and they all looked identical and were the same color. An accident waiting to happen.

On airplanes, it used to be that the flaps and the landing gear were right next to each other. If you reached for the wrong one, the landing gear would retract and the plane would just drop on its belly onto the tarmac.

When you hear this stuff, you think, how stupid can they be? But Norman will tell you—it is not stupidity, it is simply bad design.

Norman would say that his work centers on "trying to understand how the mind works" and then design for it, rather than around it. "The real danger in hiring the world's best experts is that what they create will probably be unusable by ordinary people."

I asked him about startups, and he made two points that are absolutely required—"product process" and "deep focus." He tells the story about going in to see John Sculley, then CEO at Apple, and John would tell him a great idea. Norman told him that sure, it was a good idea, but it would take 200 people two years to do it. OK, get started. And then the next day Sculley would call him into his office and give him another good idea. And so on.

Norman preaches focus. And process. And of course, Steve Jobs was the archangel of those two themes. Norman says, "The simpler a product appears, the harder it is to get it that way."

(At one point, Steve Wozniak reported to Don Norman. It was because Woz "wanted to be an employee.")

He poked fun at the infamous meme MVP (minimum viable product)—he says many young entrepreneurs "forget the word *viable*." When he was at HP, he says, "you were only allowed to take risks on projects if everything turned out OK." In thinking about user-centered design, he says, "What we are first told is the problem is usually only the symptom." You have to dig deeper to properly understand the issue. "You have to solve the correct problem."

For example, when you go to a hardware store to buy a three-fourths-inch drill bit, maybe what you really want to do is mount a picture—and maybe there is a way to do that without drilling a hole. What is the real problem?

Don Norman is 80 going on 16. He has a twinkle in his eye and a healthy irreverence for the status quo. He questions everything, and believes "that the technologists, not the academics, accomplish the breakthroughs." He is at UCSD because he wants to do "something important and exciting."

And that means he wants to expand the design universe. The two most famous design labs are at MIT and Stanford. His mantra is to make UCSD the third one.

I asked him for his final thoughts for entrepreneurs—"to make a difference, have fun." I love this guy.

RULE #454

Answer the right question.

HANDS UP FOR THE ENTREPRENEURIAL GRANNIES

FEBRUARY 22, 2016

My bride, Barbara Bry, and I vigorously preach that entrepreneurship is alive and well and global. OK, for the middle square and the win—where is Uganda?

Here is the inspiring story of Lydia Mugisha, 58, a grandmother who lives in a small village in Uganda and owns Lydia M Crisps.

She grows Irish potatoes, peels and slices them, then cooks them on a charcoal stove, packages them in polythene papers, attaches her name tags and finally, sells the finished product to customers. She controls the complete supply chain. She is vertically integrated. (No Harvard MBA, but she figured it out. Same as Apple and Tesla.)

I love this. Basic staple meets consumer demand—and voilà, a miniature potato empire is born.

She is almost 60. Entrepreneurship knows no age limits.

Mugisha's path to entrepreneurship came out of necessity. She is one of many Ugandan grannies with primary responsibility for their grandchildren because of AIDS and economic hardship throughout the country. Her initial funding of 200,000 Uganda shillings (about $58) came from Women's Empowerment International, a San Diego-based microfinance organization focused on helping marginalized women in San Diego and developing countries work their way out of poverty.

"Our focus is poverty reduction and giving women hope, self-esteem and the ability to control their lives and destinies," said Win Cox, the founder and president of Women's Empowerment, or WE.

Mugisha tells her story without emotion. "I take care of seven grandchildren. The parents of these seven children have either been killed by thieves or divorced or disappeared. It is a hard life here. So I am their lifeline." Her fierce determination is evident, but quiet. She does what she has to do.

In addition to startup capital from Women's Empowerment, Mugisha received four days of training from a local NGO, or non-governmental organization, called the International Fertilizer Development Center. Against overwhelming odds, she started and made this business thrive. Currently, her monthly revenues are about $72 and profits are $29. Just imagine for a moment the pitch deck she might present to a venture capitalist. They would love her margins—40 percent.

Her biggest challenge, she says, is not having a commercial house where she can sit and sell her crisps. She works from home and says she does not have access to adequate transportation. To grow her business, she wants to borrow money to rent a space in a trading center. The success of Lydia M Crisps has allowed her to pay school fees for her grandchildren, buy home necessities and pay for health care. She is self-sufficient. She is an entrepreneur with positive cash flow. (Tell that to a few of the "unicorns" in the Valley.)

Women's Empowerment was started in 2003 by Cox, who joined with marketing executive Jan Percival and journalist Leigh Fenly and then a larger group of 35 San Diego women. The group issued its first microloan in 2005, and the total value of loans made since then is $523,230. As loans are repaid, new ones can be made, and the total number is more than 22,000.

The group works with partner banks throughout the world and chose to focus on grandmothers in Uganda, said Cox, because "we want to serve the poorest of the poor women—the impoverished grannies, who range in age from 55 to 95, and have the impossible task of supporting their grandchildren and other orphans they are raising with little or no income.

"For most of the grannies, their bed is a dirt floor. If they have shelter, it's a hut. Their only food comes from their modest gardens. And each evening, their grandchildren must walk some distance to get water. Rainwater tanks cost $10, thus few own them. In December, WE funded $20,000 in tanks for the grannies who are the oldest and whose grandchildren have to walk the farthest, often five miles. That dusk walk is especially dangerous for young girls."

Currently, WE is making about $200,000 per year in micro-loans, according to Cox. The group's goal is to fund $500,000 per year by 2020. It is an ambitious effort.

"To do this, WE needs to transition from an all-volunteer organization to one that has a blend of volunteer and professional staff leadership. We need to be there for the grannies who are living in extreme circumstances and await a hand up, not a hand out," Cox said.

RULE #453

There, but for the grace of God, go I.

NEGOTIATING IS A NUMBERS GAME

MARCH 1, 2016

Carpe diem. But unfortunately you can only carpe this day once every four years, this being the 366th day in the intercalary year. Technically, we need to help God and his cosmic reality by adjusting our Gregorian calendar in order to keep it in alignment with the Earth's revolutions around the sun.

So, let's play around with numbers. But not round numbers. It turns out that "when negotiating a price, never bid a round number," says Matti Keloharju, visiting scholar at Harvard Business School. And he has the numbers to prove it.

People place more value on precise numbers than they do on relatively round numbers. If you say, "I will pay you $14.26 per share for your stock," you are taken more seriously than if you say $15 or $14. The amount is not that important—it is the appearance of having crunched the numbers and been rigorous and thorough and detailed and not just "ballparking" it.

(**NOTE:** Sometimes, I listen to the financial/retirement radio junk—and the free books they are sending me are always a $247 value. Enough said.)

Also, do not make a bid that ends in zero. In studying the social psychology of bidding, Keloharju went back and reviewed 2,000 merger and acquisition offers between 1985 and 2012. Of course, the investment bankers, those gods of the financial firmament, got it wrong 47 percent of the time. They bid in a round number, and the target company (as well as the stock market) was not enthused, and they did not win the deal. But when their bids were divisible by $1 (but not by $5), the success rate was over 75 percent. So, be precise; it makes you sound smarter than you are. Start to listen closely to the advertorial marketing pitches—not a round number in sight.

I recently spoke to a class of young entrepreneurs. They were charming, but a bit naïve. (Maybe that's why I got the gig.) At any rate, I polled the group and found that only a couple had read any material outside their narrow interests. I will not beat a dead horse, but please—no more TechCrunch, no more TheFunded, no more blogs or industry promotional deal-venture-unicorn-oriented nonsense. Seek a wider range of information—*Bloomberg Businessweek, The Wall Street Journal, Forbes, Fortune, The Economist, Fast Company*. You cannot be in "the startup business" if you do not expand your business horizons—and that does not mean increasing your posts on Instagram.

And this is because of a simple fact. If you are working on something in your garage, I guarantee you that at least a dozen other people in the universe are working on almost the same thing at the exact same time. Remember, it's what you don't know that you don't know that will kill you. (I am now stepping off the soapbox.)

And now a shout-out to venture capitalist Nin Desai, 2015 Illinois CEO of the year. Here are her top five qualities that she seeks in an entrepreneur.

1. Dream big with ideas that scale. But have an idea that is applicable to all (or most) industries.

2. Personality traits. Desai preaches focus and communication skills in the CEOs she backs.

3. Industry expertise. You will need some "been there and cleaned the toilets" to demonstrate domain knowledge.

4. Adaptability. She interviews using a series of "what ifs" to see how nimble the team is.

5. Choices. That is code for how you build the management team. How do they work together, what is the culture, can they get across the finish line without killing each other?

And finally, Desai touches something close to my own heart. Does your venture have, at its core, any reason to exist other than to make money? She mentions Zynga (games) and Groupon (coupons) as examples of companies that did not meet her test. She asks, "How does your company make things better?"

RULE #456

If you can do well while doing good, that's a pretty good target to shoot for.

BEING ORIGINAL CAN TAKE YOU FAR IN THE WORLD

MARCH 14, 2016

I have been to the mountaintop.

And when I got there I found my guru—not a swami, yogi, mystic or maharishi, but a 35-year-old Wharton professor by the name of Adam Grant. And folks, he is the real deal!

You need to read his latest book, *Originals: How Non-Conformists Move the World*. A year ago, I wrote about his first book, *Give and Take*, in which he proves that givers have more success than takers or matchers. And now Grant has come back with a double dazzler.

He tells the story of Warby Parker, founded by three Wharton graduate students—his students—and how they asked him to invest. In the book, he gives all the good reasons why he did not invest. And you nod along with him and agree that the company was never going to make it. And then he tells you that it was the worst financial decision he had ever made. (After all, Warby is now valued at over $1 billion—and Grant could have been the very first investor.) And then to drive home the point about "originals," he tells you all the reasons that his initial reasons were wrong. He is honest and humble. And you wonder if you would have invested if given the chance.

He argues that there are two roads to achievement—conformity and originality. One is maintaining the status quo; the other is taking the road less traveled, going against the grain.

He studies originality—and how you can spot it. Grant tells of a study that shows that the browser you use is an indicator. Firefox or Chrome users are more creative than Explorer users. They do not choose the default option.

He explains parenting. (That alone should qualify him for a Nobel Prize.) And it matters not only to whom you were born, but also in what order. The first-child syndrome turns out to not be so great for creativity and originality.

He explores Polaroid and why it failed. And he makes a persuasive case for strategic procrastination. And my favorite section (about my favorite show) is on how *Seinfeld* almost never got made. And he explains how the best venture capitalists in the world made the worst mistake with Segway.

And then there is Beethoven. Not a bad composer, so they say. But what is fascinating is that Ludwig was a terrible judge of what was great and what was ordinary. He didn't think much of his 5th Symphony and nearly scrapped the ending of the first movement. There are similar stories about Picasso and *Guernica*. But the defining characteristic of the above originals is that they produced a very large amount of work. In other words, they went to the plate a lot of times and swung at a lot of pitches. Beethoven, 650 works; Bach, more than 1,000; and Picasso, 1,800 paintings and 1,200 sculptures. Not a single "one and done" in the group.

You want to win a Nobel Prize in science? Study art. It turns out that your odds are 12 times greater if along with some science, you also write poetry, novels or short stories.

Grant measures intuition against domain expertise. And he argues that originality rarely comes from the comfort of insiders. After all, why rock the boat? And he talks about "speaking truth to power" in a strong story about a CIA operative, Carmen Medina.

And he tricks you with the "Sarick effect"—called putting your worst foot forward. Spoiler alert: there is no Leslie Sarick. Familiarity sometimes trumps rational observation. He explores "first mover disadvantage"—the difference between pioneers and settlers. Kozmo raised $250 million but failed. Netflix came second and was the winner.

Grant has a chapter on "Rebel with a Cause." Ask yourself, how many baseball players have stolen home successfully—and who were they. He has a chapter on managing anxiety, apathy, ambivalence and anger. It is better than 30 years of psychoanalysis (and believe me, I know where of I speak).

In his own words, "Becoming original is not the easiest path in the pursuit of happiness, but it leaves us perfectly poised for the happiness of pursuit."

There are dozens of discussions and programs and panels in this town about innovation and startups and creativity—stop the madness. Just read this book!

RULE #457

Just read the book.

SOMETIMES LIVING ON THE EDGE IS WHERE MAGIC HAPPENS

APRIL 18, 2016

They lower you into a large glass-and-steel cabinet—filled with water—upside down in a straitjacket, handcuffed. All you have to do is hold your breath and get out of the manacles, before you drown.

This seemed perfectly reasonable to Harry Houdini. All in a day's work, he did it more than a hundred times. I think this magic trick best approximates what it is to be an entrepreneur today. The trick is to "get out of the box." And what you need to know is that every deal starts in a box.

When I was younger, I imagined viscerally this image of holding your breath. When I started out in real estate development, I didn't have much money, so the only deals I could do were the ones that "had a lot of hair on them." That is code for deals that were so screwed up that no one really wanted to mess with them. But they were perfect for a guy with no dough and an outsized dollop of chutzpah. They were always like *The Perils of Pauline*, a last-minute escape from the tracks before the train ran me over.

One time I literally flew down to the City of San Diego's redevelopment agency with a check for $500,000 that I had to present before their 9 a.m. Friday meeting on that day or I would lose all my development rights to a high-rise that I had spent more than two years securing. I was hanging out for more money than I really had. I got the dough 36 hours earlier on Wednesday evening. I got out of that box—barely.

This image of having your head held underwater—and you simply having to hold your breath until you can figure a way to get out and breathe—is classic for the entrepreneur. I tell this story because in the past few weeks, I have witnessed five entrepreneurs get out of their handcuffs. I know every one of these chief executives personally, and I admire their skills and their lung capacity. None of them had a lot of air left to spare.

So what is it that allows some of us to get out of the box, while some of us drown?

One thing that stands out is the willingness to throw every idea against the wall—to tap on every inch of that wall looking for the loose board and the secret passage out—to be willing to be stupid, to be willing to repeat the same set of puzzle sentences until somehow you see something different.

You need the willingness to go to the stupid-waste-of-time meeting across the country, to be willing to quit, to be done with it, to admit defeat and failure and humiliation—and then somehow when you can acknowledge that you may in fact die, that you may have to really close, that there is no more money and there is truly no way out, then sometimes, resurrection shows up.

I can't explain this phenomenon to non-entrepreneurs. There are a hundred stories of meeting payroll with two hours to spare, of getting an order when it is the last day and without the order, it is over. I cannot explain how or why this happens, but I don't think it is random. I think the "entrepreneur personality" must hold a special place in heaven.

Don't misunderstand me. I have drowned more than once. It doesn't always work out. Sometimes the damn handcuffs do not come off.

But when I see success snatched from the darkest corners, I applaud. It is magic. And I adore magicians (have seen Penn & Teller five times, as well as all the Las Vegas magic shows, and have been to the Magic Castle in Los Angeles). I love the illusion. I don't believe my eyes. It can't be. He can't catch a bullet in his teeth.

This is the startup game. Hold your breath long enough to escape drowning, then pop to the surface and with a flourish create the illusion that brings them to their feet.

RULE #463

How did he do it?

MODERN PLAGUES AFFLICT OBSERVANT BUSINESS TYPES

APRIL 25, 2016

I am Jewish.

Not the most religious, but still a regular attendee at synagogue, I am celebrating the eight days of Passover. This is God's revenge on the Jews, who are forbidden to eat bread as well as 129 other things that are tasty to remind us of the misery that our ancestors endured in Egypt under the evil reign of Pharaoh (sometimes referred to as the first venture capitalist).

The story is a simple one told by historians. They tortured us, we fled, the Red Sea parted, and then we had a really good pastrami sandwich on corn rye. But first, we needed a hero—Moses. God tells Moses that he has been chosen to free the Hebrews from slavery in Egypt. It is reported in one of the books of the Bible that Moses responded, "This 'chosen people' thing is getting a bit tiresome; would it upset your grand plans if you chose someone else?"

But God has a plan, and he sends 10 plagues down to help soften up Pharaoh and get him to see the light. I offer to you the same plagues—but with a modern interpretation.

1. Blood. The waters of Egypt become polluted and unusable. For reference, visit Flint, Michigan.

2. Frogs. This comes from the famous line "you have to kiss a lot of them." This means presenting your pitch deck to 83 investors who are only tire kickers, while looking for the one guy who actually owns the car.

3. Gnats. These are your pesky LinkedIn/Facebook friends who tell you how cool you are, but really only want a job.

4. Wild Animals. These are the very large gnats.

5. Pestilence. After you have been jerked around by investors, suppliers, customers, partners, co-founders and employees, you are inclined to say, "Fie, a pestilence upon you all." Trust me, that is a rational response. You will be forgiven.

6. Boils. This was designed specifically for all the Jewish children who were demanded by their pushy parents to become doctors, and when they graduated from medical school, instead of choosing neuro-micro-genetic brain surgery, picked dermatology.

7. Hail. Biblical scholars often misinterpret this plague as the cry when you are trying to get a cab in New York on a rainy night after the theater. If it is cold outside that night, then you get hail.

8. Locusts. This is sometimes interpreted to mean consultants. This plague afflicts startups who do not have a fully formed management team and are promised a safe passage across the Red Sea if only they will enter into a six-month, non-cancelable monthly contract for services, which in retrospect will be seen as superfluous and useless. (They tell you that the water is wet.) Consultants can be spotted by business cards that contain words like "take your business to the next level"—and the frequent use of the word "strategery."

9. Darkness. This is that period between the day after the first raise of money for your company and the day before the last day when you either go broke or sell the company. During that time, there is only darkness. Beware the darkness. (See #4 above; wild animals will be in some of the cubicles.) Buy a headlamp.

10. Death of the firstborn. God is getting pretty serious at this point. No happy board meetings now; you missed your numbers, your burn rate is too high, you have no sales, your CFO quit, the code doesn't work and no one cares that your app will connect space aliens to shoppers at Whole Foods for free delivery of food using SpaceX. This one is why I still go to synagogue.

But do not lose hope. There are always things that happen that you cannot plan for and often appear when you least expect it. Moses drags the gang down to the Red Sea—the only way out—and the surf is above their pupicks (Yiddish for belly button), drowning is definitely in the cards—but as they enter the water, the sea parts and they walk across on dry land. Some people would call it the result of global warming; I call it a miracle.

RULE #465

Don't question cosmic events; just be grateful.

GO TO THE PROPER SOURCES TO CONFIRM YOUR BRIGHT IDEA

MAY 2, 2016

"I have an idea." Great, you don't say, "Wow, how cool."

Now the problem—is it a good idea? This of course is the critical piece of thinking. Determining if an idea is good is not easy. And, who should determine the idea's true value—the creator or the manager? The answer, according to Justin Berg, a professor at Stanford Graduate School of Business, is neither.

Berg studies "creative forecasting"—aka the skill of predicting the success of new ideas. Think of technology of course, but then think of books, entertainment and real estate development. Think of every little guy who starts a business and believes he has a good idea.

What Berg finds is that the best judges of an idea are "the peers of the creator." He reached this conclusion by studying circus acts. He interviewed 338 circus professionals and had them watch videos of new circus acts to determine which ones they thought would be loved by the audience. Then he tested that against 13,000 audience members.

Managers tended to undervalue the most novel ideas. They opted for the more conventional acts. But the other performers— not the actual creator of the act but other "circus people"—were more attuned to what would actually work for the audience. The best judges were their peers.

"Creators focus on idea generation, while managers focus on idea evaluation," says Berg. He explains the difference between "divergent thinking," which is how creators search for new connections, and "convergent thinking," where managers use previous knowledge as the baseline of what will work.

So, obviously, the takeaway here is that you need to build a company in which there is significant cross-pollination among the various skill sets. While the computer geek may not have an MBA, there is a very good chance that he or she will recognize a breakthrough and its significance before the business development guy.

I experienced this in a biotech in which I am involved. The significance of one of their tests was not apparent to the team until another scientist in a different field in a different city pointed out to us what we had. It changed our direction in launching a diagnostic product. The "peer" was a physician who was better able to see the novel aspect of a technology that the creator team had not fully appreciated. We had something, but we were looking at it from the wrong direction.

(**NOTE:** Don't worry about someone stealing something— especially if you don't even know what you have is worth stealing.)

Of course, one of the most famous ways to test an idea is to go talk to your customer. Spend some shoe leather and leave the office to find out what the customer wants.

The only problem with this is sometimes you don't know what to ask. And that is because the new idea may not have gotten out of its incubation in your company, potentially squashed by the manager who did not give it enough air so that you could even show it or discuss it with the potential customer.

The other puzzle here is how much time and money do you spend on exploring a new idea before you kill it or feed it. The limiting factor is time. You can't chase every idea, so you need a process to better pick the winners. To that end, Berg has one last thought: Talk to the "hybrid"—the guy who was a creator and moved to manager and so knows something about idea generation.

Think about baseball managers and football coaches—almost universally they were former players. Venture capitalists are often former chief executives of successful companies. So the "been there, done that" service stripe has some credibility in moving up the managerial ranks.

On the other hand, the fact that you can write brilliant code does not translate that you can manage 100 engineers or sell software services. Beware of letting employees rise to their own level of incompetence and find themselves in a cave of their own making with no way out.

Ideas are a dime a dozen. Now if I only had to spend a dime to find out which ones are really good, I would be very rich.

RULE #461

If it's such a good idea,
why are you showing it to me?

LET CHILDREN EXPLORE LIFE AND LEARNING
MAY 9, 2016

The Wall Street Journal has pushed my button. Rant on!

On May 2, the Small Business section had the following headline: "How to raise a tech entrepreneur," written by Alexandra Samuel. Are you kidding me? Have we come to this, where the only thing that matters in this whole world is another "tech entrepreneur"? Is there even room (perhaps just a small Airbnb room, just a closet or a tent, maybe) for someone who might, possibly, have an interest in something other than tech—maybe, for example, theater, art, film, science, medicine, geology, health—or is the only thing that could possibly have any value in America ever again another tech entrepreneur?

And God forbid that you don't teach your child early. Because Harvard be damned, after all, he is going to drop out in his freshman year anyway. But if he misses out on becoming a tech entrepreneur, he will be a failure and spend a lifetime living in poverty on the streets or in a homeless shelter, using food stamps and regretting that you deleted Instagram from his phone when he was five.

The lead paragraph of the article begins, "Everybody wants to give their children the tools to be a success in life ... but think big for a moment, how could you prepare a child to start the next billion-dollar tech company?"

I did not make that sentence up. It is the lead. My question is, who would want to? Has the entire human existence and its future value (Excel will calculate the net present value) on this planet come down to starting another unicorn (many of which lately have been a bit "de-horned" in valuation)?

Here are her words: "Have them embrace computers and social media as early as possible." Of course, after all, there is no future in sports, music, architecture or wandering in the woods (Thoreau). When I was seven, I built a ham radio set and as many of you know, I am still talking to aliens.

Samuel encourages your child to build a website (today all you have to do is add water), and she goes on to say, "Here are the strategies to raise children with a shot at the next rags-to-tech-riches story." As you all know, that is the main purpose of having children. Happiness is vastly overrated.

So her strategies are: "Raise problem solvers." Every complaint is a learning opportunity. You don't like dinner? Well, darling son of mine, what kind of food would you like to invent? "What would your dream restaurant look like?" Maybe she is prepping the little tyke for celebrity chef.

Samuel goes on to say parents should teach the child to "identify serendipitous opportunities," but of course that assumes that the kid got his nose out of the computer screen long enough to learn what *serendipitous* even means.

"Get them social media savvy—before they turn 13. They have to grow up inside the social networking universe." (Snapchat meets Bubble Boy.) Samuel wants children to begin using project management software to track homework and family tasks. But caution here—big data will know that your son cannot hit the curve ball, and unfortunately he will still be picked last by his peers on the field. But all is well, because there is a therapy app for low self-esteem.

She goes on to say, "Teach children to work like a start-up." I assume that means either 90 hours at your desk (take out the trash yourself, Mom—I am competing in a coding hackathon) or free organic lunches followed by yoga and a beer bong Friday blow-out.

"You're much more likely to produce the next Mark Zuckerberg if you get your children to start their own ventures at a young age." I am sensing that dinner at the Samuel house would include a PowerPoint presentation and then a short discussion revolving around either liquidation preferences, selecting an investment banker for your IPO or eat your damn green beans, darling.

She proudly states, "My daughter started her own Etsy store at 7." I am inclined to call child protective services and have this woman committed. Listen, I love the entrepreneurial spirit—I went around the neighborhood sharpening knives at 10. But please, let's stop the madness. A child's life should allow him to look at a cloud, not to be stored in one.

RULE #467

There is no app for the meaning of life.

NOT TO GET TOO SAPPY, BUT PEOPLE WORK BETTER HAPPY

MAY 23, 2016

Happy, happy, happy—yuk.

Happiness is big business, and it is studied incessantly. Papers on happiness are published in *Science* magazine, people who study happiness win Nobel prizes, and everyone wants to measure just how happy you are.

Happiness in the workplace really matters. Daniel Gilbert, a Harvard Business School professor, has done some studies in this area. "Employees are happiest when they are trying to achieve goals that are difficult but not out of reach," he says. This reminds me of my yoga teacher (or any trainer), who pushes me hard, but not so hard that I pick up my mat and walk out. Namaste to you, pal. The lesson here as a leader is to set goals that can be reached—but not too easily.

Gilbert points out that we "synthesize" happiness—which is code for we always find silver linings, and we have the human desire to make lemonade out of lemons. If you go blind or lose a fortune, he says, "you'll find that there's a whole new life on the other side of those events." (Listen, Gilbert, I'll take your word for it.) He says you would learn to be just as happy as you were before—before your wife divorced you, took the children, moved to Arkansas, bought a pickup, fell in love with a rodeo rider, and got a good lawyer who took you for 89 percent of your assets. Gilbert promises that you would find a way to smile.

So now let's take happiness (or the lack thereof) into the entrepreneurial office. Are contented employees the most productive employees, or is it better to keep people a little uncomfortable, a little anxious about losing their jobs? (Think Steve Jobs, Jack Welch, etc.) The studies are clear. Challenge and threat are not the same thing, and reward and encouragement always work better for your team.

Is frequency of positive experiences more important than intensity of them? It is the little things, the dozen small things on a regular basis, that really set the happiness barometer. That argues for pizza on Fridays, rather than a massive, expensive Christmas party. Gilbert tells you to kiss your partner, sneak a french fry, wear comfortable shoes, and your productivity will increase. (The problem with happiness is that it is obvious—but elusive.)

Another big idea on happiness is that it is "moment to moment." Humans calibrate their happiness hundreds of times a day, and small stuff (whether annoying or satisfying) has a big impact. One of the researchers, Matt Killingsworth, has built an "experience-sampling application" called Track Your Happiness. It queries you multiple times per day, checking on your emotional state. Killingsworth is exploring not if you are happy, but rather "when you are happy."

On a personal note, I had breakfast recently with an old friend, an investment-banking analyst, and he looked great. He said he was happy. Turns out he had given up drinking, cut up his NetJet card, started yoga, stopped yelling at his wife, sold his race cars and is leaving his job, which he hates. Duh.

I can tell you that I spend a lot of time at my various companies checking on people's happiness. I can actually see if they are not happy—it is obvious—and my job is to figure out how to help them get to a better state (without medication).

Talk therapy has benefits; train yourself on how to listen.

It is incumbent on the CEO to set a culture of happiness. I know that sounds goofy, but it is real. Encourage social interaction (volunteer at a homeless shelter), practice gratitude (I know we are going broke, but not for another five months), support exercise (the team softball nonsense seems to work). One of the most selfish things you can do is to help others. It will make you happy. (Unless you are a short, Jewish neurotic, but that is a tale for another time—on the couch.)

RULE #466

"It is the very pursuit of happiness that thwarts happiness."

—VIKTOR FRANKL

NETWORKING AND OLD-FASHIONED SERVICE

JUNE 13, 2016

Potpourri week.

Networking: I still go to a lot of networking events, and I am always surprised at the outcome. Invariably, I meet four or five interesting people. I get their business cards, and then I religiously send an email the next day reaching out in some way.

One of my most recent events was a mix of millennials and old folks at a fancy La Jolla mansion. The speaker was a Zen guru who wanted us to be more holistically in touch with ourselves … yada yada. But only one of my reach-outs returned an email. There are lots of possibilities, including that I am just not as interesting as I think I am, but in general, the rule remains—return every email and every phone call. You just never know for sure, and ignoring is never a good opening move. (After all, that is why you went to the event.)

Marketing: I got a very fancy and expensive card on the door at the house offering a high-end, concierge house-cleaning service. The previous day I had decided to fire our current service. First thing I learn is that I can only access them online. I had to fill out a form, and they would get back to me.

This requiring an email inquiry seems to be the de rigueur way to capture information. My question: Whatever happened to a telephone number? I find it often impossible to find one on a website.

I filled it out and waited. No word. I am a fairly relentless individual, so ultimately I found a phone number and called, was put on hold for nine minutes, and eventually a person answered. I asked if I could speak to the owner about services because I wanted to hire them.

Her response was, "I don't know the owner. We are a call center in Nashville."

Now, here is the kicker. That evening when I got home, I placed a call to the owner of our current service asking if we could talk the next day (but in a tone that suggested there were some issues), and then I settled in to watch the Warriors game. Thirty minutes later the doorbell rings and it is the owner of our house-cleaning service—at my door and wanting to know the issues and not going to wait until the next day. We talk and we resolve, and I am so impressed that I end up offering (he never asked) to increase the fee I pay. There is no substitute for customer service. No substitute, period.

Coaching: It seems I am late to this game, since there are already hundreds of people in this line of work. I have recently begun to take on a small number of coaching clients. To that end I revisited Anders Ericsson, the Florida State professor whose new book, *Peak*, explores high performance and expertise.

He says, "Just working harder does not seem to be associated with high levels of performance ... rather it is working with a mentor or teacher who can help you." I have spent a couple thousand hours in psychotherapy—and I can tell you that you can't see the pimple unless you have a mirror.

Ericsson is most clear on one point: "We know that in order to get benefits from training (or coaching) you need to be fully concentrated." I think this argues well for a set time period. In the case of therapy, it is usually 45 to 50 minutes. My coaching session is never more than 75 minutes. Because after a certain amount of time, you just can't apply "concentrated" focus any longer. Golf lessons are often 30 minutes. Longer is not necessarily better.

And this argues for companies to create "training environments" in which employees are actively engaged in a highly focused learning moment, but for a compressed period of time. If you want confirmation of the above, talk to your personal trainer—heavy weights, very few reps.

Darkness: That is when your company is in extremis. I recently watched the movie *The 33* about the Chilean miners trapped underground who survived for 69 days. And then I re-read *Endurance*, the book about Sir Ernest Shackleton. These stories bring light to the darkness.

RULE #469

There is no substitute for leadership.

BIG DECISION? MAYBE THE WHITEBOARD WILL HELP

JUNE 27, 2016

The two people I most want to have dinner with are Sigmund Freud and Daniel Kahneman. I want to ask Siggy when is a cigar just a cigar. And I want to ask Danny boy why people make stupid decisions. Freud is not around anymore, but Kahneman is—and he has some thoughts on that subject.

"I look at large organizations that are supposed to be optimal, rational, and the amount of folly in the way these places are run, the stupid procedures that they have, the really, really poor thinking you see all around is actually fairly troubling," so saith the guru.

As most of you know, Kahneman is a Nobel laureate, and is considered to be the father of behavioral economics—the study of why we make the stupid decisions we make. Here are some nuggets from a recent lecture.

One theme is that we make decisions in a way that is not "commensurate with the complexity and importance of the stakes." I see this in my own little companies. Decisions get made off the cuff, by the seat of the pants, or by gut instinct. To combat this, I will often stand up and say "this decision really matters" to call attention to its significance. Wave your arms, light a small fire—make sure the team knows that this one has big implications. In other words, slow down the rush to judgment. But that still doesn't mean you will get to the right decision.

Kahneman says that human beings are hamstrung by "overconfidence, limited attention and cognitive biases." In other words, we tend to jump to conclusions. We want to tie up the loose ends and complete the narrative before we get halfway through the book.

And he says we are highly susceptible to "noise." His use of that word implies that our decisions are random and unpredictable. He did a study with radiologists and found that about 20 percent of the time, with the same X-ray, they get a completely different diagnosis.

Kahneman also studied financial institutions (now, that is a rich vein indeed for stupid decision making) and found that decisions involving hundreds of thousands of dollars frequently hinged on the opinion of one individual. And when Kahneman presented the exact same set of facts to different groups of financial decision makers, their conclusions varied between 40 and 60 percent. In other words, half the time, at least half of the group had their head in a different cloud. Wow, tell that to Mr. Dodd and Mr. Frank.

And the topper is this one. Novice financial decision makers had as much variation as experienced professionals. In other words, your loan approval is a toss-up. Now multiply this into the hundreds of millions and apply it to the world of investment bankers, and you understand why 40 percent of M&A deals get unwound within 36 months of making them. (You gotta love those bankers; they come right back in and flip it again for some new fees.)

So the solution is—algorithms. Kahneman is clear: "The indications are unequivocal. . . . When it comes to decision making, algorithms are superior to people." Data dictates. And here is the best part: "It does not require a massive amount of data. . . . Make a list of five or six dimensions, give them equal weight and you will typically do better than a very sophisticated statistical algorithm." (Who needs big data? Small seems to work better.)

One of my companies recently had a really big decision, a life-death decision that would impact the entire company and its future. Three of us sat in a room with a whiteboard for three and a half hours. We listed four options, and within those options, we reduced each to only two variables. When Kahneman talks about an algorithm, he is really talking about a mathematical decision process—a weighted set of "what ifs" coupled with a decision tree of outcomes A or B or C for each. (And it appears that we got to the right decision; the company is still breathing.)

In the end, for each decision process, he also adds a "global rating." He calls this his concession to human intuition—the gut thing—and it turns out that the global rating was highly accurate, more than any of the individual assessments alone. But, that correlation could only occur after "the exercise of systematically and independently evaluating the constituents of the problem."

RULE #471

Love the whiteboard.

EVERYONE'S TRYING TO BE AN ENTREPRENEUR

JULY 18, 2016

The fierce, clear-eyed, young startup entrepreneur who has set out on his own course to shape a new reality and create innovative technology and bend it to his will. This is the myth of the new John Wayne shaping the West (side of Silicon Valley).

Not exactly.

I have been puzzling of late over the "everybody is or wants to be an entrepreneur" syndrome. *Fortune* magazine had a headline last year, "At Harvard, Wharton, Columbia, MBA start-up fever takes hold." At Kenan–Flagler at the University of North Carolina, "40% of the class of 2015 are studying entrepreneurship."

And when it comes to fever, our own little river city does not have to take a backseat to anyone. Recently, I attended a CONNECT biotech event and it was jammed. The most recent Start-Up Week event had more than 750 people. There is a new collaboration between UCSD and the Downtown Partnership focused on startups. Everyone is working one room or another.

I think back to the movie *The Graduate*, wherein the magic word for the future was "plastics." Today it is "startup." If everyone is starting, are there any people finishing? It feels like there is a sense of franticness in the air. Remember the Gold Rush—the only guys who got rich made the shovels and the jeans; they did not dig for the gold.

To this end, I offer some thoughts from the book *Invisible Influence* by Jonah Berger, a Wharton professor of marketing. He writes about "how others shape our behavior—often without us knowing it." He tells the story about his lawyer dad buying a BMW and then lamenting that every other lawyer in Washington,

D.C., had a BMW. The son says, "Well, Dad, you bought a BMW also." The dad responds, "Oh, but mine's a blue one. Everyone else drives a gray one."

Social influences are much stronger than you think. This is true of clothing, cars, homes, careers, etc. And it is the whole idea behind "things going viral." Viral is the equivalent of a monster wave trying to shove you into the shore of tweeting and buying and thinking, and according to Berger, you are mostly powerless to resist.

An example of positive power of the social influence is when you ride your bike in a group versus alone. In the group (the peloton) you go faster. This is "social facilitation"—it matters who your friends are and what they do. (Tons of research on this about gangs and violence.)

Back to the BMW. It is a good car, so why shouldn't I buy a good car—just because Bob Jones has a BMW doesn't mean I shouldn't have one. But trust me on this, when you buy the BMW, you will think of yourself as being different from just keeping up with Mr. Jones. This is called being "optimally distinct." It is also a self-delusional con. You are not that different; you just think so.

Berger also looks at motivation. How does the mere presence of someone else affect your own performance? (He says it is more difficult to parallel park when you're on a busy street and cars are backed up waiting; on a quiet street, you kiss the curb and get it right the first time.)

So is the entrepreneurial fever mostly fed by the Internet and the world around us, and if so, is it perhaps time to take an antibiotic? Personally, I am conflicted. I love the game, and I am still playing it. But I have no illusions about being unique.

Maybe my concern is that there are too many new members who have joined the club. That is the "I liked the band before everyone else knew about this cool band"—and now I have to go find another band.

Berger uses a line from *South Park*: "Oh, you can't be a nonconformist if you don't drink coffee." In the end, I support and applaud the entrepreneurial spirit—but be aware that your choices are heavily influenced by unseen forces, and resisting is pointless. The storm is going to carry you out to sea. Just be sure you take a PFD with you—personal flotation device.

The best line from the musical *The Fantasticks* is from Luisa: "Please, God, please, don't let me be normal."

RULE #775

Nonconformists conform just as much as everybody else.

WANT TO GO INTO BUSINESS? TRY GETTING A Ph.D.

AUGUST 1, 2016

Theranos. Where was the "science"?

I will not take the opportunity to exhibit unreasonable schadenfreude, notwithstanding that Elizabeth Holmes (note here that she is not Dr. Holmes) was a Stanford dropout, with a penchant for secrecy and a quasi-delusional mind meld that conflated herself with a fellow named Steve Jobs. She also possessed a keen sense of self-promotion, having assembled an august board of advisers, including Henry Kissinger and George Shultz, two men who had exactly zero knowledge of biotech blood diagnostic discovery. And to top it off, not a single "name-brand, tier 1 VC" was an investor. (Need I remind you of the risks that come with "dumb money"?)

Her personal net worth, once valued at $4.5 billion, is now closer to $4.50 since she has been scorched (the legal term is "suspended and sanctioned") by the FDA and banned for two years from the drug lab industry. As a note, Hollywood, never one to miss a chance at an Icarus moment, has signed Jennifer Lawrence to play Holmes in the to-be-made movie. So enough grave dancing; the cemetery is crowded.

What I want to discuss is the power of the Ph.D.—doctor of philosophy, which in its original incantation refers to "a lover of wisdom." *The New York Times* recently ran a long piece by Gina Kolata, in which she points out that we have such a surplus of science Ph.D.s that only one in six have a chance to get a tenure-track position at a university. And if you get one, then you live and die by the grant industry. In other words, you desperately want a job in which you have to find your own money to pay yourself and your post-docs, and your chances of getting a grant are now 40 percent less than they were in 2000.

Talk about eat what you kill, wow.

A friend of mine (a Ph.D. in molecular biology) recently wrote a blog post in which she suggests that a science Ph.D. is not only good for work in a lab. She argues that the training can be cross-utilized in corporate leadership roles. At Valeant (the stock has gone from $240 to $22 in 11 months), the non-science CEO famously said, "Don't bet on science, bet on management." He has recently been removed.

In the case of Theranos, the visionary leader had no science background, yet she wanted to change health care in America. Admirable indeed, but a little chemistry might have proven useful.

"It used to be that the majority of Ph.D.s in the biological sciences would go into an academic career, and now it is very much the minority," says Michael Lauer, deputy director at the National Institutes of Health. Using current hiring statistics, Lauer goes on to say that "84 percent of new Ph.D.s in biomedicine should be pursuing other opportunities."

And as for the post-doc, he is told "your job is to work for your professor to help him succeed." Talk about the 18th century in Britain and Germany, where indentured servitude was the only way to get out of Dodge. My friend goes on to say that the scientific training that comes with a Ph.D. includes a large amount of public speaking and presentations, analytics, defense of ideas in a peer review setting and regulatory awareness—all of these being useful skills in management.

I have run a few companies with wickedly smart Ph.D.s, and I can tell you that their business skills were excellent. Maybe they can't describe a stock derivative or a sinking fund or a broad-based weighted average stock dilution, but their leadership and their probing and their evidence-based assessment of reality was quite strong. Their training proved to be the check and balance to ego, money and obfuscation.

The idea here is that perhaps the Ph.D. track is a bit closer to an MBA than once thought. The substance of the work is clearly different, but the skills might be translated across enemy lines.

The world of the science Ph.D. who can only see academia as the endgame is dark. The competition is fierce and rejection is the norm. But take your degree into industry and the corporate world, and things begin to brighten. Hard science and hard work can indeed change the world, not with arm-waving self-aggrandizement, but with rigor, detail, curiosity and passion.

RULE #474

Love the test tube, but don't marry it.

SECOND CHANCE BLOOMS BEHIND BARS
AUGUST 8, 2016

Lancaster, California, July 23, 2016: 109 degrees.

Location: California State Prison—CDCR (California Department of Correction and Rehabilitation)

No, I was not headed to prison as a potential inmate (I know there may be a few folks in town who are disappointed to hear that). I was there as part of Defy Ventures, a program designed for inmates to "become the CEO of their new life." And without any equivocation, I can tell you, this day was transformative, as much for the inmates as for the volunteers.

Meet the life force behind this project—Catherine Hoke. This lady is electric, and what she has achieved with the Defy program in five years is amazing. She describes Defy as blended learning. The program includes 150 course hours online and over 3,000 volunteers who range from the Valley elite to Harvard MBA professors to regular chuckleheads like yours truly. Google has given a $500,000 grant, and 100 startups have been founded and funded since the inception of the program.

Hoke describes the program as "Khan Academy meets Y Combinator—but for people with criminal histories." Like many entrepreneurs, she had a strong father, a Hungarian inventor who challenged his children "to invent something in 60 seconds" at the dinner table. She says, "I have always been a contrarian." She was the oldest of four children, competed on the boys' wrestling team, played women's rugby and then went to UC Berkeley. The youngest undergraduate ever hired by a venture firm in the Valley (they wanted her to be a deal originator), she worked in venture and then in private equity in New York. And then she took a trip to Texas.

That trip was fateful. She saw the Texas prison system and decided she could make it better. You have heard many times about the entrepreneur who wants to change the world—but mostly what they really mean is they want to build an app and flip it and make some serious coin. Not Hoke. She actually wanted to change the world.

Now when you want to change the world, and the world you want to change is filled with tough guys who have committed serious crimes, you need some street cred. Hoke has the stripes and scars that earn her their respect. You can read her story, but bottom line, she made some mistakes, she admitted them, and then in the good-old-boy world she lived in, they fired her. And that became the impetus to go back and make it better. (Or as I like to say, beat their brains in.)

I have lots of rules in my book, but one of them is right on the money with this woman. "The reason that entrepreneurs do this is not for fame or fortune, it is for revenge." She was going to take a serious whack at the prison system and how it can better prepare its population for a life when they get out.

Defy has been in business for five years. It has graduated 175 EITs (entrepreneurs in training) who went from being "in training" to real life, with a less than 4 percent recidivism rate. Wow. And I can tell you if Hoke ever comes back in another life, she should audition for Marine drill sergeant. She is fierce.

I wanted to experience this event up close and personal, so I dragooned my pal Mark Bowles to come with me and spend the day at the California State Prison.

Let me tell you about the day.

First, it is a real prison—Level IV. Maximum security. I asked Hoke about it in an earlier conversation. She kidded me by calling it "Attica West." I am not so sure she was kidding.

Razor wire, slamming steel doors, massive security—just like television, except I couldn't change the channel. Built to hold 2,500 inmates, its current population is 3,500, or two prisoners per cell. There is the mandatory de-briefing, of course. The prison warden, Debbie Asuncion, does the usual welcome, and then there is one line that significantly gets my attention. She notes that "if any of you are taken hostage, we will not negotiate for your release." You can't make this stuff up. There are five very large guys in front of us who she assures us "will make sure we are safe." My time lecturing at the Miramar Brig is going to seem like a walk in the park compared to this.

Thirty volunteers had signed up for the day; 17 showed up. Hoke does not like people who don't do what they say they are going to do. Most entrepreneurs feel the exact same way.

We walk across the prison yard—and then it is unbelievable. The door to the facility opens and in front of us is a gauntlet of 55 prisoners—cheering. Our job is to run down the line and high-five everyone. The inmates cover us with stickers, just like you see on football helmets. There is more cheering and music. If you walked in a bit uptight, by the time you get down the gauntlet, all pretense is gone. You are a homey and in the trenches now.

These EITs have been working on their "new life" for three months, and this was the halfway point in their program—meeting the volunteers. In another three months, they will participate in a mini shark tank with their ideas for the chance to win a portion of $100,000 in funding.

Next, there is some rap music, there is dancing, there is vulnerability, there is tears. There is one exercise that nearly breaks my heart. Hoke lines the inmates up on one side of a line, the volunteers on another. Then we all step back and she calls out questions and if it applies to you, you step up and toe the line.

"Finished high school"—only one-fourth of the inmates step up. All the volunteers do, of course. "Finished college"—one inmate out of 55 stands on that line. If you don't think education and crime are related, stop reading.

When asked about who is in for murder, about 80 percent step to the line, same for life sentence (but with the possibility of parole). Abused, single parent, drugs, early "loss of innocence"—and so it goes. It is heartbreaking to see that nearly all of them are on the line now. You really begin to get a sense of who these people are—and you get a bone-numbing, gut-wrenching awareness of what it means to be white and privileged.

The day is packed with interactions and reveals. You hear loss and pain and regret, but you also hear hope and the possibility of a future life. And what I hear deeply and consistently are personal statements about regret, sincere apologies and a fierce commitment to have a new life and never to do that stupid thing again.

I believe in second chances.

The inmates have workbooks and written materials, they have resumes and they have prepared and memorized "personal statements." The goal of that statement—that beginning when you tell someone who you really are—is not to get the job; it is to get the interview. Break the puzzle down into pieces.

At the end of the day, Hoke asks for money, naturally. What I had told her previously was that Bowles and I would give money, but only for a program in San Diego to support one of our local prisons.

So now comes the shameless challenge. I ask Hoke how much it takes to do the program at one of our prisons (Donovan is a good choice), and she says I need a two-year commitment, and the total cost is $100,000 ($50,000 per year). That is enough to serve 100 inmates per year, so a total impact for 200 inmates. I tell her I will see if WE (that means you) can get that done.

There is an enormous amount of talk about mentoring and incubation and innovation in our community, and I want to channel some of it, right here and right now, to the less advantaged. These inmates are not computer science graduates from UCSD, their goal is a barbershop or a food truck—but I assure you, if you ever get your hair cut or eat a taco from a Defy Venture graduate, your life will never be the same.

If you have an inclination to donate, send me an email for details. I am opening an escrow for Defy/San Diego—be the first on your block (not cell block).

RULE #475

Think about it.

WHEN IT COMES TO POWER, HOW DOES THE CEO USE IT?

AUGUST 22, 2016

Power is defined as the ability or capacity to direct or influence the behavior of others. Or as Lord John Acton said: "Power tends to corrupt and absolute power corrupts absolutely."

These are interesting political times, and so I have turned to the Stanford Graduate School of Business (giving Harvard a rest) for some insight on this from Brian Lowery, a professor of organizational behavior.

"If life focuses on the pursuit of happiness (ref: Declaration of Independence), then work focuses on the pursuit of power," he says. (I am not sure I agree with his thesis, but let's give him the benefit of the doubt.) I have been thinking about power in terms of one's network. The famous phrase is "it's not what you know, it's who you know." How does a CEO "influence" his team without appearing to be a dictator giving commandments? (Steve Jobs and a few others are exceptions to the rule.) What is it to have power and then to wield it?

Lowery posits six sources of power.

Reward. You have power if you can give a reward—think salary, title, authority. My instinct is this is a modest power, meaning if your developer doesn't think the raise is enough, he is outta there and another job is waiting. So the employee has power as well. Consider increased stock options.

Coercion. This works well in prison, but I do not think it is an enlightened way to lead in normal circumstances. Once again, the employee has power. This might work well with the TSA at the airport, but the millennial generation is not much inclined to blindly follow by dint of any threat. You are then in the box of having to make good on the threat—which might be extremely counterproductive to your company.

This is the problem of unintended consequences.

Information. Say hello to Washington, D.C. Who is on the inside and who is not is the currency of power in the Beltway. I see in my companies a distinct movement toward ultimate transparency in management. Think about the customer service agent at the airport when your flight has been canceled (like my most recent airplane flight)—that is power.

Legitimate. It used to be that parents were "entitled" to tell or guide or discipline their children—because they were the parents. They had legitimate power. Not anymore. This one went out in the 1980s.

Expert. This is a big one.

If you are building a company and only Harriet Smith knows how to load-balance the network, she has the power. That is the fantasy of the service provider. They are purported experts—except there are a multitude of them, so their information is widespread and not proprietary. But the power of the rainmaker lawyer—the one who knows the cellphone of Vinod Khosla—OK, that is real power. He may not be an expert in corporate security law, but he holds the potential key to your financing and that phone number is going to cost you.

Referent. This is a fancy word for celebrity, for fame, status, charisma. It is the whole worldwide media of people who are famous for being famous—and thus are often asked to give their opinions on subjects about which they know nothing. But they have an entourage—and the entourage has power by mere degrees of separation.

The above categories are interesting, but what moves my personal needle is not power but persuasion. I want to lead by giving the compelling argument, by reasoning with enough rigor and skill that the direction I am asking the team to follow becomes "obvious." And there is nothing unique about my thinking—all CEOs aspire to these themes.

Lowery also worries about "inappropriate behavior" when you have power. For that, just google "stupid executives having affairs with their secretaries"—no shortage there.

My instinct is that power is constantly in flux and that executives often "overplay" their hand. There is the famous leadership/negotiation mantra of knowing when to "draw a line in the sand"—OK, hotshot, but when the other guy walks over that line, your only option may be to take your shovel and pail and walk away.

RULE # 505

"Power tends to corrupt and absolute power corrupts absolutely."

—LORD ACTON

EVEN SMART INVESTORS SOMETIMES GO ALONG

SEPTEMBER 12, 2016

Why are we so stupid?

I am intrigued by the demise of Skully, the San Diego motorcycle helmet maker with the augmented reality–embedded screen. They raised over $10 million from investors and took in over $2 million in pre-orders through Indiegogo. What happens to cause a company to implode? They had 1,900 pre-orders, and they shipped fewer than 100 helmets. You can read multiple points of view on the Internet, ranging from product inadequacy to malfeasance. I am not giving an opinion, but the question is a larger one. Why is it so hard to see a train wreck approaching?

Think about Theranos. Elizabeth Holmes was on the cover of over 22 magazines, blond, black turtleneck, attractive and ready to change the world, but after $400 million invested capital, lo and behold, they had to confess that the technology didn't work. And amid allegations of fraud and malfeasance, Ms. Holmes was banned for two years from running a diagnostic lab.

An investor does due diligence in order to make a rational INITIAL decision, but then what keeps him from understanding and monitoring and reviewing subsequent decisions and deliverables? (And let's tell the truth: some investors' idea of due diligence is no more than a cup of coffee at the corner with the pitch deck hovering above the pizza slices.)

I am in a deal where we were promised the moon, they said they could build it—and to date, no product, and we have simply written it off. Now here is the dark sentence: I was distrustful from day one, but I did not prevail. Where did I fail? What kept me from being assertive and squashing the whole thing before we had written a check?

Because I was not positive—and because I wanted to hope and "we wanted to believe." In retrospect, it was fairly obvious. How come I could not see it, and if I could, why did I acquiesce? Go along, get along—most people would not ascribe that phrase to me, but still I didn't stamp my feet and demand rigor.

One answer is that drawing a line in the sand is an all-or-nothing move. If you are right, no one really likes you (arrogant snot, thinks he knows it all) and if you are wrong, you are out the door. And revisionist history is a fool's errand. Tell it to the judge while you stand in line at the unemployment office. Being right and being rich do not always follow one another.

Play it safe. The mantra used to be "no one loses their job by picking IBM." But if you go with a hot startup and they fail, you are dead meat. I am a believer in the Black Swan effect—an unexpected event of large magnitude. Stuff happens. But the key here is that what you think is an outlier happens much more frequently than you would anticipate. And we try to rationalize it, and we concoct explanations, *after the fact*, in an effort to make the events explainable and predictable.

Shudda seen that coming.

For example, no one saw the 2008 financial implosion, but by 2010, there were 15 books explaining it. A lot of good that does. As individuals, we tend to look back and analyze, rather than look forward and strategize. Your company is fragile; you need to make it "robust."

Why do startup companies with no revenue and an unfinished product think their pre-money valuation is $10 million? What are they smoking? Do they listen to anyone, or do the founders/insiders get blinded by greed and stupidity, unaware that it is the next round when Jesus comes around to preach the gospel?

And finally, let me quote Salim Ismail (*Exponential Organizations*): "The concept of ownership works well for scarcity, but accessing or sharing works better in an abundant, information-based world," which is an elegant way of saying that going it alone today is dumb. There are more than a dozen separate nonprofit programs or institutions (from UCSD to Evo to the Downtown Partnership to Connect to Rady to Biocom and beyond), along with over 17 "technology incubators," all chasing limited dollars (scarcity). Wouldn't it be logical to work together for the betterment of the city and the technology community in the aggregate, rather than serving us the recycled pablum of the evil twins—ego and stupidity combined?

RULE #478

Other than that, Mrs. Lincoln . . .

LUCK IS A POWERFUL FACTOR IN MAKING PEOPLE RICH

SEPTEMBER 26, 2016

"I won the ovarian lottery."—Warren Buffett

What the Oracle of Omaha is saying is that he won the lottery when he was born white, healthy, smart and living in America. Right before he exited the womb, there were 6.8 billion tickets, and he was lucky enough to pick that one. And Buffett is very public about his blessing. He says, "Gratitude is a key ingredient to personal happiness."

But this column is not about inequality or privilege or education or race or gender—it is about luck. What role does luck play in making you rich?

For this, we turn to Ben Steverman at Bloomberg Businessweek. He tells the story of Robert Frank, who had a heart attack on the tennis court. He lives to tell the tale and play again because there was an accident three blocks away at that time, and two ambulances arrived, and only one was needed, so when the call came, the extra ambulance reached him in three minutes. The rest is history. No double fault.

Frank, who is a professor of economics at Cornell, says, "I am alive today because of pure dumb luck." Not sure if it was coincidence or divine intervention, Frank has now begun to study the role of luck in the creation of wealth. His new book is *Success and Luck: Good Fortune and the Myth of Meritocracy.*

Frank boldly reminds us of a bit of political heresy. He points out that Elizabeth Warren and Barack Obama were "pilloried" for suggesting that "the wealthy among us didn't do it all themselves." The Masters of the Universe howled.

Frank rightly points out the role of the individual, the Bill Gates, the Steve Jobs—they were talented and hardworking. But they happened to arrive at the same time that a favorable macro environment arrived.

If you bought a house in 1990, you entered a favorable macro for 15 years. Same as buying stocks in April 2009; the Dow has almost tripled since then. Think about how you met your current wife (assuming you are happily married). Twenty minutes on either side, and you probably miss each other.

Not only where you were born, but when you were born make a difference. Kids born in the fall tend to be the oldest in their class. That has a relevance that gives these children a lifelong advantage over their peers. Lucky sperm club.

And finally the dark sentence is this: the fierce economic competition in all areas today tends to favor the "winner take all" result. The few top performers reap the bulk of the rewards.

Look at venture firms. Ninety-five percent of the massive returns come to only a very few firms. So the goal for every fund is to be in those deals—at any cost. But there is only room for the most favorite—and success breeds success, so the little guy does not really have a chance.

And the Internet trumps (sorry about that) geography. You can dominate your industry from a cabin in Montana—if you have Wi-Fi.

Frank runs a simulation in which he inserts luck as a component of just 2 percent. In other words, skill is 98 percent of the result. But with 100,000 participants, "the most skilled person wins just six percent of the time."

Let's also look at my favorite Nobel Prize-winning economist, Dan Kahneman. "The world is far more random than we are programmed to believe," he says. "It is always easy to make sense of one's life in retrospect." Kahneman has done a study on Wall Street traders and found that their results were actually not much better than random selections. It made them crazy, but "there is a great deal more luck than skill involved in the achievements of people getting very rich."

Very is a key word. It is the outlier result that is disproportionate. If you had a software company in 1999, you were very lucky.

Frank goes on to explore tax policy, suggesting that if we provided more opportunities for everyone to get lucky, we would create more wealth across all sectors. "Would you rather drive a $120,000 Porsche on a well-maintained road or a $300,000 Ferrari over one with deep potholes?" (I leave that puzzle for the next election.)

RULE #480

Never discount the power of luck.

SHOULD YOU TRUST YOUR GUT IN MAKING BIG DECISIONS?

OCTOBER 10, 2016

How good is your "gut" at making important decisions?

When John Coates was a researcher at Cambridge University, he decided to study "whether gut feelings were merely the stuff of myth or something real" by looking at traders on Wall Street. Did they do better when they did weeks of analysis and due diligence, or when they shot first and aimed later? Coates was not just a researcher, he was a former trader at Goldman Sachs and Deutsche Bank.

Coates focused on physiology, heart rate, back pain, stomach upset, sweat—monitoring the vital signs. In an earlier study, he saw that there were distinct physiological signs of distress during market volatility, but the traders did not believe they were at risk. In other words, their bodies were sending out red alerts and their brains were ignoring them. Like having four drinks in an hour and assuming you're good to go in the car.

A famous trader, George Soros, relied on "animal instincts." He used the onset of acute back pain as a signal that something was wrong with the portfolio. I am fascinated by analyzing risk/reward. So Coates set up an experiment. Using heart rate monitoring equipment, he asked a group of traders to silently count their heartbeats without touching their chest or pulse—and then a control group who were not traders to do the same. It turns out the traders did much better at monitoring, they were more attuned to their heart rates—and here is the kicker: when Coates went back and looked at their trading records, the ones who counted the most accurately were also the ones who produced the most profitable trades.

Now let's muddy the water a bit. Gut instinct is not the same as intuition. Harvard professor Eric Bonabeau has written a paper in which he states, "Detached from rigorous analysis, intuition is a fickle and undependable guide. In highly complex problems (i.e. the more options you have to evaluate, the more data you have to weigh) the less you should rely on intuition and the more on reason and analysis."

But we love the myth of the gunslinger (*The Magnificent Seven*). The "push all the chips into the middle" guys like Fred Smith (FedEx), Michael Eisner (green-lighted *Who Wants to Be a Millionaire*), Andy Bechtolsheim (first investor in Google, with no legal piece of paper). They trusted their gut. But of course the playing field is also littered with vastly more corpses of people who died like dogs having bet the farm based on a feeling—and ended up homeless on the streets of Laredo.

Bonabeau says, "The romance of the gut and listening to the subconscious makes us feel special. After all, any idiot can run the numbers, but the gift of a good gut—that is reserved for the true business elite."

The answer is nuanced of course, because if you listen to your gut AND you run the numbers, do the hard work analysis, but check your heart rate, do yoga for your back and study pattern recognition, your chance of getting it right—well, I default back to my favorite economist, Dan Kahneman's, book, *Thinking, Fast and Slow*. There are times for both. Not the most satisfying answer, but probably the right one.

UPDATE: Regular readers will remember the column in early August about Defy Ventures and the Donovan State Prison project.

You, gentle readers, contributed over $30,000 (ranging from $25 to $5,000); the VCs in a Van gang (me and three pals) contributed $40,000. The big gun was Union Bank Foundation, with Kathy Patoff at the helm, which pledged $50,000. The Donovan management team met with the Defy team at the prison and then at my house, and prospects for the program look bright. We will continue to keep you posted in this column.

RULE #482

If it were obvious, we'd all be millionaires.

COACHING MILLENNIAL WORKERS: FINDING THE COMMON GROUND

OCTOBER 24, 2016

I do some executive coaching, and while most of my paying clients are not millennials, of late, I have begun to consider mentoring some of the younger folks—and it is a challenge. So to get guidance I turned to David French's article in National Review, "They're Delicate as Snowflakes but Not So Harmless."

French starts with a story about a debate at Brown University this past year. The subject was the "alleged campus rape crisis" with two opposing views being presented, and the next day, Brown set up a "safe space" on campus to help students recuperate from the intensity of the debate. In this safe space, there were coloring books, cookies, Play-Doh and videos of puppies. (I am not making this up.) The course description in the catalogue was retitled "Coddling 101," a two-semester course. Required material includes bringing your own "blankie."

The secondary theme of his article is that these snowflakes are not spontaneously generated; "they are formed largely by parents who have loved their children into the messes they have become." The confusion in the parent-child syndrome of late seems to be a tilt toward "being friends with your offspring"—and this carries through to their early employment opportunities.

And the final theme of his article is that these very same millennials are hyper-aggressive, polarized, filled with anger and very unwilling to compromise, and act in a hostile manner toward ideological opponents. To get attention, they protest and attack and seek conflict.

When they were children, they screamed as loudly as they could for Mom and Dad. But these very same millennials can no longer turn to their parents to enlist their support to rage against the machine; they are now in your workplace, and instead they come to you with their anger and disappointment and laments of unfairness. I have to be careful here, because it is easy to say "suck it up and get back to work," but I am only partially of that school of thought. I am more inclined to try listening and to see if I can turn their anger into profit. But listening is not abdicating, and "I am not your pal, I am your boss" is a sentence that managers often have trouble saying.

In classic jujitsu, you turn the opponent's strength and weight against them to disable their attack. The challenge for the manager vs. the millennial is to channel their anger into a force for good without being dismissive of legitimate concerns. Several of my companies have a healthy dose of millennials, and by and large, I love them. Wickedly smart and creative, but sometimes they can make you crazy—saying things such as "I need a better title," or "Can I attend the executive management meeting? I want to listen." The executive coaching programs in the business schools need to offer a course on the care and feeding of millennials.

If you and your co-founder are both very similar in age and orientation, then there is much less conflict as you begin your company, but in mature companies, the search for the common ground is often not so common. The manager is often left with only two choices—"my way or the highway" or abdicating and marginalizing in order to keep the peace, the equivalent of kicking the can down the road (in political speak). Bob, weave, deflect and keep going.

Look, we all know that corporate culture is subtle. You can't buy it with venture dollars, and there are countless stories of leaders being unable to work together or leaving "to pursue personal projects" or more bluntly, getting fired. French says, "The fragile generation will either exhibit greater aggression as they flail for the utopia that can never come, or have a rediscovery of the virtue of perseverance." The authority figures in the company (the management) cannot guarantee enduring joy and success. The Tiger Mom can't go to school with her young.

For us older folks, learning how to motivate and energize the younger worker is not just foosball and pizza; it is finding a place to dance that mixes our waltz of the cotillion with the hip-hop of the aughts. Our job is to hear the music, and then, uninhibited and unembarrassed, we need to move our two left feet to the beat.

RULE #484

If you want a friend, get a dog.

WHITE-COLLAR CRIMINALS ASSUME THEY WON'T GET CAUGHT

OCTOBER 31, 2016

I recently perused some files from the Criminal Division of the United States Attorney's Office for the Eastern District of New York and found this exchange from a hearing in Judge Horatio Blotzburger's courtroom.

Prosecutor: The State alleges that you conspired to fraudulently steal over 239 million dollars and accuses you of trading on insider stock information, of running a Ponzi scheme, of penny stock manipulation, of embezzlement and of sex trafficking for personal gain. Did you do all these things?

Defendant (Mr. Usvoq): Yes.

Prosecutor: Why?

Defendant: I didn't think I would get caught.

Prosecutor: Is that the only reason?

Defendant: No, I had a difficult childhood, my father was mean, I have low self-esteem, I am defined by my net worth, I am incapable of deep human emotion, I need to be the smartest guy in the room.

Prosecutor: Were you surprised when you were found out?

Defendant: Well, yeah. I mean I had a nice home, lovely wife, good kids, a great salary, served on multiple nonprofit boards, was held in high esteem by my peers—frankly, I was a big shot. I had the plane and the boat. And to tell the truth, I just didn't think the laws applied to me.

Prosecutor: What about the pain you caused your victims?

Defendant: (surprised) Huh, just didn't cross my mind.

Why They Do It: Inside the Mind of the White-Collar Criminal, by Eugene Soltes, professor at Harvard Business School. This is a must-read.

Given my current interest in criminals (Defy Ventures and my sojourn inside the maximum security prison at Lancaster), I was fascinated by Soltes's book. He interviewed four dozen prisoners—including Bernie Madoff and Allen Stanford (Ponzi schemes), Scott London and Sam Waksal (insider trading). The book dispels the idea that "most corporate crooks are masterminds who carefully calculated their illegal acts, weighing the risks and rewards." In fact, it is exactly the opposite; they didn't plan even one chess move ahead. They simply assumed they wouldn't get caught.

Soltes also finds that many of his subjects exhibit "an overwhelming lack of remorse—these men are really good at rationalization." And further, there is a disconnect in their minds between a violent crime and financial fraud.

I recently spent another full day in prison witnessing a "shark tank" business plan pitch by the EITs (entrepreneurs in training). I will spend some time on that in a future column, but what is overwhelmingly clear is that every one of these men is fully and completely remorseful. They are working through their shame, they are deeply aware of the pain they caused and viscerally affirm that they will never do that again. I looked into some very deep and dark souls during my day in prison, and I think the contrast that Soltes paints about empathy is powerful.

Soltes tells about Steven Hoffenberg (Ponzi for $475 million), who viewed his operation "not as a deceptive criminal enterprise, but rather as a pragmatic issue." He wanted the money. And he, like all of them, created a tight little box. He stole during the day and came home at night and kissed his wife and children. There was a complete disconnect.

The white-collar criminal can intellectually understand that he has hurt people, but it appears to not resonate emotionally. But here is the kicker. All of us are susceptible to these cognitive biases. You and I think that because we have a good moral compass, we are immune to the disease—naïve and wrong. What Soltes suggests is that all of us are capable of rationalization and compartmentalization. After all, everyone is going 20 mph over the speed limit (everyone steals), so I will also. Easy to catch the germ; it's blowing in the wind.

Finally, Soltes points out a partial solution—seek input from other people outside your bubble. You need someone to push back on your assessment. In his case, he usually turns to his wife (a physician)—"she sees the world very differently than I do."

(NOTE: The first part of this column is completely made up. And for those of you who are hackers out there, who is the defendant?)

RULE #506

Who, me?

PICKING ONE CANDIDATE OVER THE OTHER IS TASK AT HAND

NOVEMBER 7, 2016

Today is November 7. Soon our long national nightmare will be over.

But before we turn out the lights on this one, let's find a bit of wisdom from one of my favorite Harvard Business School professors, Clay Christensen, and ask (of both the candidates and the American people), "What job did you hire that product to do?"

Christensen's new book is *Competing Against Luck: The Story of Innovation and Customer Choice*. In this book, he explores why people pick one product over another. And of course, the American people have some choosing to do. So the question I want to ask is this: What job did you hire the product to do?

Christensen says, "When we buy a product (the president) we are 'hiring' it to get a job done. If it does the job well, we hire the same product again. And if the product does a crummy job, we 'fire' it."

Well, that might be true for vacuum cleaners, but it seems that politics might resist that rational explanation—because some jobs are not just functional, "they have critical, social and emotional dimensions." In part this explains why some companies demand huge loyalty (Coke, Facebook, Nordstrom), as well as the current phenomenon of rallies—where large numbers of previously-thought-to-be-semirational people yell things like "lock her up."

Christensen says that when you take a new job, you are not only being hired, but you are hiring the company. True enough, but in the case of American politics, at best you are only hiring 52 percent to 54 percent of the company—the remainder hate you.

Christensen goes on to talk about happiness (I have been in therapy a very long time, and I can tell him that categorically happiness is only attainable in blocks of time measured in nanoseconds), and his theory is that lack of happiness is the result of a "fundamental misunderstanding of what really motivates us" (not taking off your shoes when you get on Air Force One isn't enough). He says that just because you are not dissatisfied with your career path doesn't necessarily mean that you are satisfied with it. (Sure, go try to prove a double negative.) He says we are driven by "intrinsic" factors, not just the perks in a new job. He asks three questions.

1. "Am I being challenged and learning in this job?" Well, learning the nuclear codes is not that easy, and finally getting out of Iraq will be like getting 2400 on the SATs.

2. "Am I respected by my peers and my boss?" Dude, I am the boss, but that respect thing, I am not so sure. Why are they filing articles of impeachment?

3. "Does the company have a mission I truly believe in?" Whoa, that mission thing is my responsibility, but getting 100 senators and 535 congressmen to go along, that is quite another matter—the only thing harder would be two on the aisle for *Hamilton*.

Christensen talks about interviewing candidates for the "Jobs to be Done." He wants to figure out if the candidate has the right fit. In his Theory of Jobs, he explores the concept *why would anyone in their right mind want to work here?*

Put differently, if you want to be president, you should not be allowed to run. You can't work remotely; your vacations are interrupted by terrorist attacks; you have to give press conferences (very few if you are lucky), where rabid journalists looking to make a name for themselves ask you questions about your bathroom habits or your email, claiming that they are of national interest and the company (that's us) has a burning right to know.

Can a job provide long-term happiness? Not if you have to reapply for it every four years. We, the company, love certain products, but I think what we really love is the blood sport of actually picking the products. After we buy one (from Amazon, delivered by a self-guided drone), we get bored. The presidency is like a box of Legos—fun to open, but after you make a cat and a dog, you lose some of the pieces, and who needs another version of the *Millennium Falcon*—we'd rather watch a rerun of *The Walking Dead*.

But we are the company and we pick the job to be done—but this job is unlike any other. You can't be sure, there are no guarantees, but don't give up, don't phone it in—vote with thought and care, but vote.

RULE #507

How could this happen to America?

(NOTE: This rule was written on November 8, 2016.)

FITTING TOGETHER THE PIECES OF MAKING A GOOD DEAL

January 30, 2017

When is "no" no?

Let's meet BATNA—the Best Alternative To A Negotiated Agreement. We folks here in San Diego have just lived through a mutual BATNA with us and the Chargers.

Harvard Business School Professor Jim Sibenius has some thoughts on the subject. According to Sibenius, the essential idea is to evaluate any possible deal by a simple criterion—"as compared to what." It is natural and necessary to weigh the alternative. "The reason you negotiate is to produce something better than the results you can obtain without negotiating." San Diego's BATNA will emerge over the next few years—and I am quite optimistic (166 acres is not chump change). This will now conclude any further references to the Chargers.

On to the deal business—where I make my bagel and butter (which is my BATNA to a croissant). The BATNA concept for negotiation is very powerful. For example, take a reasonably content married couple who are at loggerheads over a significant issue. The options range from "yes, dear" to divorce and all the stops along the way. In all cases, it is likely that they will have to interact with each other for a period of time (children), so caution in figuring out their BATNA is important.

I am on the board of a software/food delivery company which is about to receive a significant investment from a venture capitalist. My CEO is concerned that some of the "tech world buzz" on the firm is less than stellar. But if we don't take the money, we go broke in four months, although my CEO says that maybe we could get some more angel money. Bottom line here seems to be take the VC money and run (and stay in control of the board of directors).

In another company of mine, we walked away from a complex deal—without an alternative readily available. In that case the BATNA was to take our chances and hang out—six months later a white knight showed up. Had we taken the other deal, it would never have happened. In that case, delay worked on our side, our cards got stronger during the interim, and the market caught up to our technology.

"Continuing to negotiate" is a tactic. You don't a draw line in the sand, but you keep making sand castles. A BATNA should not be seen as "the last resort." Long before that time, you should have found a place you can live. And sometimes when there is no good option, you can try the "strategic no" and threaten to fall into the arms of their fiercest competitor.

I am a consultant to a company where the "founder" is intractable. There is no communication and no negotiation. And of course they are running out of money. So in this case my job is to convince said founder that his BATNA is to settle. Failing to get a calm rational behavior agreement, I will recommend we "put on a black hat" and fire up Louie the Litigator—welcome to cram down, pay to play, common stock conversion, fiduciary—you name it. Throw the book at him, and the hope is that he will see that his BATNA is to get in the boat and row. I need to create leverage. How do I explain that it is better to be in the boat (albeit in the back) than it is to drown in the ocean?

With another company, I am currently battling a tech transfer office, (not my favorite UCSD), and in this case, my job is made more difficult in that the gentleman on the other side is doing his first deal and wants to "make his bones." I need to explain that his BATNA is simply to not lose the deal. Our founder/genius/ scientist is a famous-in-her-field rock star, and if you continue to act like a jerk to prove to your bosses that you are a tough guy, we will disappear and you will be remembered as the guy who let her get away.

Sibenius concludes with the three kinds of rejection: A "tactical no" (floating a test balloon), a "no to reset" (i.e. no for now, but let's meet in a couple weeks and try again) and "a final no" (drop dead, you dog, die and pound sand).

RULE #495

With wives, "yes dear" is a sure winner.

EMOTIONAL QUOTIENT IS KEY TO CAREER DEVELOPMENT

February 6, 2017

"What can I tell you—the guy just seems a little 'off,' not really clueless, but sometimes the dude just seems to have two left feet."

I will wager that conversation has occurred more than once in your business interactions. The factor that you are aware of is called Emotional Quotient (aka emotional intelligence). EQ plays a major role in your career advancement—even more than your achievements. In any group, there is always someone who "gets it." He/she makes everyone feel comfortable, moves the ball without dropping it, has a glib and friendly manner, senses when to talk and when not to talk, and knows how to defuse awkward moments. In other words, the person has a high EQ.

So to learn more, I turned to a new book, "Unequaled" by James Runde, a former Morgan Stanley investment banker. I need to tell you that being a successful banker is about 93 percent soft skills and schmooze and 7 percent number crunching (which you get the junior grunt just out of Wharton to do for you), so this guy knows whereof he speaks.

Runde says that when associates were not promoted in the bank, the stumbling block was usually one of the three things that are required to be a banker. (I can't help but hear echoes of the famous "Seinfeld" episode where Newman gets a speeding ticket in his effort to save Kramer from suicide, his misery brought on by his failure to become a banker).

The three things that either limit or doom your advancement are "lack of adaptability, not good at collaborating or just didn't click with clients." In other words, the candidate did not create empathy with the client. Runde explains that these three skills—cognitive, work ethic and emotional intelligence—are critical in dealing with clients. Now every B-school in the country can teach the first two, but the third one is not so easy. There is no algorithm for EQ. It is like fuzzy logic (where the truth values for the variables are exactly that—variable.)

What advances a banker's career are networking and bringing in the clients—and that last one, above all, requires the client to trust you. Trust. I have some pals who do "wealth management," and the sad truth is that most of their investment returns are within 50 basis points of each other up or down. The way they keep their clients (even when they pick a dog that goes down 60 percent) is that you, the client, have developed a trust in them. And EQ and Trust are intimately tied together.

Runde hires MBAs right out of school. The first transition he demands is from the academic case (teacher knows the right answer and you learn how to parrot it back to him) to the business case (there is no right answer and you need to figure it out). The additional subtext here is that in order to advance his career, our young associate also needs to find a "sponsor"—not just a mentor. His upward arc depends on hard skills, as well as a sponsor who gets him into the right place at the right time—takes him along on a big deal, gives him the ball with a relatively clear field, so he can score. (Finding a generous sponsor is a whole other ball of wax—and EQ is primary for that one.)

Runde says, "It's almost like kindergarten. Needs to work and play well with others. The big firms do not want a lone wolf; they need a team player." (In another column, I am going to extol the virtues of the rebel in a company.)

I am not a big fan of investment bankers. They always seem overpaid to me, but when they are good, they are very good (credit that to Henry Wadsworth Longfellow). All of us need to develop empathy for the client, stand in his shoes (and then sell them to the highest bidder), as well as develop a way for clients to trust you.

This trust thing is nuanced. I think it comes from active listening, blended with a touch of humility and sending the message of comfort. It is the combination of "I will take care of everything, don't worry, it is all going to work out fine" along with "if the guy doesn't agree, we will just burn his building down." Maybe Tony Soprano should have been an investment banker.

RULE #496

Trust, but verify.

— A RUSSIAN PROVERB

FIRMS NEED REBELS WHO CHALLENGE THE STATUS QUO

February 20, 2017

"Hey Johnny, what are you rebelling against?"

Johnny (Marlon Brando in the movie, *The Wild One*): "Whadda you got?"

In a previous column I noodled about EQ—emotional quotient and its importance in getting ahead in a company. Today, let's look at rebellion straight up. If my parents and teachers were still around, they might have some thoughts here.

Once again, I turn to Harvard Business School professor Francesca Gino, who has studied conformity. (It seems there is a lot of it.) She says, "Employees are often asked to check a good chunk of their real selves at the door." Surprisingly, this attitude cuts across both big and little companies—even startups. The desire to fit in seems universal—even to the point that in an experiment where paid actors consciously picked the wrong answer to a simple perception problem; 75 percent of the group agreed with the wrong answer—just to fit in, even though they knew the correct answer. That shows the power of social pressure and its support of the status quo.

Another risk to conformity is that we often interpret data "in a self-serving manner" to support our biases or the group think of the moment. We look for a way to find a solution that supports what we already think. When an investor does due diligence, he is often predisposed to find a way to invest or not invest—but not necessarily based on the actual hard facts.

Gino interviewed more than 1,000 employees and less than 10 percent said they worked in companies that regularly encouraged nonconformity. Her solution is to encourage "constructive nonconformity"—what might be called going against the crowd. Gino actually uses the phrase "deviant behavior." Be very careful here; the theme is really to speak up with your best truth, not to just agree.

Slightly off-kilter behavior (outside business norms) seems to engender a perception of higher status. Wearing a hoodie and jeans seems to have worked for Mark Zuckerberg. And some CEOs go with red tennis shoes, and some old guys wear baseball caps.

The big idea is to encourage and support challenging the accepted model. I often challenge my various teams with the phrase "let's pretend." I know that we all think that the reality is one way, but let's pretend that something could be different—then "what if."

What a company should want is an employee who is in touch with "her authentic self." One of my favorite scientists keeps little furry animals that represent various molecules on her desk. I love it.

Leaders should tell employees what needs to be done, not how to do it. (That one is pretty basic.) Another principle in support of nonconformity is to push decision making down lower in the management stack. Think Four Seasons and Southwest Airlines— where employees are not only empowered but demanded to solve problems in real time.

Find a way to encourage employees to "bring out their signature strengths"—the area where they excel. Consider rotating people into various positions; this is a way to discover hidden strengths and capabilities. The net result is that employees feel more committed to the company, and they are more confident in their abilities.

The elephant in the room is finding a way to strike the right balance. There is a thin line between anarchy and chaos on one side and freedom within rational boundaries on the other.

At my first company, our product was a kiosk to connect to the internet in public places for your email (this is 1996). We were slowly going broke, even though we had customers. One of our junior engineers went to La Guardia airport to do an install of eight internet kiosks, and on the way home on the airplane, he had an idea: why not put the software into hotel rooms. The business traveler was going to need connectivity. He came up to my office to tell me his idea and the rest is history. We sold the company for over $80 million two years later. The best idea did not come from the management geniuses—it came from a regular guy in the field. I would call him "my favorite rebel."

RULE #498

"I rebel, there I exist."

—ALBERT CAMUS

CONCLUSION

I hope you have enjoyed the read.

I am always looking for great ideas, so feel free to send me whatever you think will move my needle.

neil@blackbirdv.com

Also, I have begun to do more executive coaching, so if you have a CEO (or are one) who you think might benefit from some time with me, once again, feel free to lob it in.

I try to answer all inquiries. If I fail, please be generous of spirit and forgiving. It is the nature of man to be less than perfect. But we all keep trying. That is what makes the game interesting and valuable and compelling.

Thank you again.

Best wishes,
NEIL SENTURIA

RULES

ACKNOWLEDGMENTS

In the matter of acknowledgements, I am anxious to call out a few friends and allies.

To CHARLES McSTRAVICK, who did the layout: All I can say is thank you, your skills are awesome.

To DON HOLLIS, who did the cover design: Well, this one takes more than one sentence. Mr. Hollis and I have been working together since 1987. He did all the work for my real estate developments, all the work for the eight companies I ran as CEO or co-founder, much of the work for the various companies I have invested in and much of the work for *I'm There for You, Baby: The Entrepreneur's Guide to the Galaxy*. I have seen him blossom and his talent and his style and his demeanor are superior. If you can hire him for anything in this area, do it.

To LISA WOLFF, who did the copyediting, my extreme thanks. I know that the editor makes the author and for this I am grateful.

To DIANA MCCABE, who is my editor at the *San Diego Union Tribune*, where these columns have appeared every Monday on the front of the business section, mostly lower right, sometimes above the fold, but always lovingly edited and supported.

To my children, RACHEL, ETHAN, SARA, and RACHEL, without whom I could have retired ten years ago. I am grateful that you are still willing to put up with the old man's stories and wanderings, along with his impending drool cup.

And finally, ah yes, finally, to KARLA OLSON. Unfortunately, for someone who prides himself on being a wordsmith, I am shucks plum out of words. She is the BOOK SHERPA OF ALL BOOK SHERPAS. No one can come close to her care and feeding and thought and warmth and vision and service—no one! This book is Vol. 3. She did the other two, and I cannot live without her. Add to that her other passion—working for Patagonia—and you have the complete human being. Wow!

I used to be in the movie business. I am a fan of Marty Scorsese; most of his films are edited, by Thelma Schoonmaker. He will not work without her. Steven Spielberg uses Verna Fields repeatedly. The point of this being when you find someone who makes you better than you really are, do not let her get away. For me, one of those is KARLA OLSON; the other is my wife, BARBARA BRY.

Ms. Bry is famous and successful in her own right, so my telling you how appreciative I am would be redundant in this respect—I am just massively grateful that she once, in a moment of miasma and euphoria induced by laughter, agreed to marry me (and then stay married) and then for the past 24 years be my partner and my muse. How does one acknowledge the other half of oneself? Thank you, BB.